Promoting Decline:

Obama vs. America

By Scott Wheeler

Capitol Media Group, LLC
344 Maple Avenue West #375
Vienna, Virginia 22180

ISBN 978-0-615-66216-9

Printed in the Unites States of America on acid-free paper that meets the American National Standards Institute Z39-48 Standard.

Acknowledgments

Many people contributed to the effort of this book. Particularly I would like to thank Angela Wheeler. Also particularly Rick Rush, Peter Leitner, Andrew Madden, Marc Morano, Nicolas Chandler, Quentin Cantu, D. Bass, and Al Checchi.

About the Cover:

Special thanks to Oleg Atbashian for cover design.

> "America is the beacon of light in this world. Obama's actions are destroying it. His attempts to bend the beacon to match the shifting, declining landscape, are breaking it because this beacon rests on timeless, absolute values—a foundation that doesn't change with the party line or on a whim of the current ruler."

> -- Oleg Atbashian

Introduction

Barack Obama. Hope. Change. Obama for America. The man isn't a leader; he's a catchphrase. It's all politics. Understandable. But what happens when the manipulations go beyond presenting yourself as a vaguely optimistic symbol for white guilt and devolve into actual, nation-betraying deception?

Is it possible that Americans have elected a president whose corruption and dishonesty are so bold and pervasive that despite the evidence before them they still cannot accept it? Obama pushed through his signature legislative accomplishment, the Affordable Care Act, under the pretense that it was absolutely necessary due to the chicanery of insurance companies. Obama's repeated chorus: "This year, they will be banned from dropping your coverage when you get sick. Those practices will end." Obama pounded those words into American heads over and over again in the lead up to the passage of the unpopular bill. Which all sounds nice and comforting to the average insured until you realize it was an outright lie. Dropping someone's coverage because they "got sick" has been illegal in all fifty states for at least two decades. And yet, somehow, this went entirely unreported by the so-called mainstream media (my column being the lone exception). What Obama had stated hundreds of times in arguing the need for his pet piece of health legislation was such a bold faced lie that had it been uttered by a licensed insurance agent he could have faced criminal charges for fraud.

As if the lies weren't enough cause for alarm, Obama has effectively used his shady double-talk to increase his power. His healthcare bill alone gave the federal government (and its chief executive, Obama) control over fifteen percent of the U.S. economy. Deception and outright lies are at the core of Obama's strategy, not only to win elections, but also to centralize control over the entire domestic economy. While robbing American citizens of their domestic power and hording it in the White House, Obama has managed to diminish the power of our nation abroad by weakening our strategic military and intelligence defenses. Why would Obama try to globally weaken the nation for which he seeks unprecedented authority to control? Perhaps this is the confluence of narcissism and anti-Americanism.

Regardless, if Obama is not actively promoting the decline of America, how do we explain why he trusts the world's most violent nations with the same military might which he seeks to deprive from his own nation? It cannot be the ludicrous belief that our unilateral disarming will "set an example for the world" and cause rogue nations such as North Korea and Iran to follow our lead, or inspire nations seeking validation of their corrupt tyrannical leadership through military power such as Russia and China to divorce their ambitions. At best, Obama's reasons for weakening the U.S. militarily are dubious, at worst treasonous, but, regardless of motive, his actions are very dangerous.

Obama's ongoing attacks on those he dubs "the wealthiest among us" (also known as the most productive members of our society) also reveals a troubling pattern of dishonesty. He arrogantly tries to portray himself as financially successful and implies that he has done something to earn it. That too is a sham. We have witnessed him time and again peering out over a crowd of followers. Hiking his chin, he looks down his nose at his devotees with the arrogance of a fraternity freshman looking over the rest of the student body after just crossing over, Obama arrogantly proclaims "I don't need a tax cut." He pretends that he has actually earned his place in the esteemed class of American millionaires. But most of this class is made up of the entrepreneurs, producers, and those who have built, created or invented; people who had paid a price and earned their way through great achievement.

Sadly, Obama had never built or created anything, his specialty had been tearing things down a la Saul Alinsky. However, he did spin a decent yarn about himself in <u>Dreams from My Father</u>, or as some suggest, talked domestic terrorist Bill Ayers into spinning some of his yarn for Obama to call his own. But this book was no great piece of literature; it was of little interest to anyone until Obama was elected to public office. It's easy to brag that you don't need a tax cut when you didn't do much to earn what you have, or risk any capital to do so. Obama had no wealth until he was elected to the United States Senate, and then, in four short years he managed to accumulate six million dollars. Unlike most other millionaires, Obama's small fortune is owed entirely to his winning the political lottery, and like other lottery winners he now considers himself a high-roller, self-qualified to lecture people who actually earned their money that they should be turning more of their money over to the federal government like he says he wants to do. When talking about his influence fortune, Obama sounds a lot like Orwell's character Napoleon the pig in Animal Farm. As the pig assures his barnyard subjects that even though he eats the preferred diet of milk and apples while they go hungry, he really doesn't like the taste of milk and apples.

There is also an Orwellian essence of economic deviancy consistent throughout Obama's speeches, statements and the way he has governed that should raise many questions about his true intentions. He uses straw man arguments to legitimize his demand for more control over the nation's resources and more power over its citizens. That deviancy was prevalent in his 2009 so-called Stimulus Bill, which used tax dollars to pay back the financial supporters of his campaign, which flies in the face of his numerous lectures to us about "fairness" and "playing by the same rules." Obama's statements are surreal considering the shocking use for which he put Americans tax money, examples of which are laid out in this book.

But the crony-capitalism, or as it should be called, crony-socialism, is only part of the story. We can't forget Obama's attack on national security which has left the nation less safe, his mobilization of the media to attack American citizens, his support and funding of the Occupy Wall Street demonstrations, and the despicable way Obama, the Democrats and the media attempted to blame the shooting of a U.S. Congresswoman on their political opponents.

And what about the opposition party? The casual political observers may ask "how can Obama get away with so much with the Republicans waiting to pounce on his every move?" This is a canard. Elected Republicans have never held Democrats accountable for anything. Even in the late 1990s, as Democrats wailed about the Republican controlled House of Representatives' impeachment of then President Bill Clinton for lying about molesting a White House intern, there was a concurrent, lesser-known congressional committee investigating Clinton for selling national security secrets to Communist China. At the conclusion of that investigation, Republicans dutifully sealed most of those files for decades, shielding the Democrat Clinton from public scrutiny over what would have been the biggest story of the twentieth century. As reluctant as Republicans have been to tear down Democrats in general, they are even more terrified of Obama. Because questioning Obama's ethics not only invites evisceration by the liberal media, it also means being branded a "racist".

The corruption within and surrounding the Obama administration is too vast for one volume to cover, but this book can start the illumination of how Obama is promoting the decline of America.

Table of Contents

Part I

Weakening National Security

Chapter 1

An Odd Choice for Openness

Obama has declared war on America. From the beginning of his term he has talked about gearing up to fight anyone who disagrees with him. He can be unequivocal about his intentions at times, such as when he exhorted Hispanic voters to "punish our enemies" in an interview conducted on a Spanish language network just before the 2010 elections.

Soon after being inaugurated, Obama called some of these "enemies" out by name: Joe the Plumber, Rick Santelli and, of course, Rush Limbaugh. Limbaugh, according to the Democrat strategy of marginalizing anyone who disagrees with them, is the leader of the Republicans. The Democrats needed to put a face on their straw man, someone to represent the conservative Americans that they attacked, and so they picked Limbaugh because they saw an easy target. Someone who is on the airwaves fifteen hours a week will surely say things that can be taken out of context, twisted and then used as examples of conservative insensitivity. It's the Left's favorite play, find something, even if only remotely provocative, pretend to be offended, manufacture outrage, and demand that elected "Republicans" distance them- selves from their supposedly "divisive" base of supporters. Being tied to an "offensive" statement by an unrelated person on the right happens all the time to conservatives; but Democrats can smear Republicans, conservatives and patriotic Americans constantly, without evidence, and the so-called "mainstream media" never bats an eye. When Limbaugh quipped that he hopes Obama will fail, the Obama administration and the rest of the Democrats exhausted the line to claim that conservatives had a personal vendetta against Obama.

Ignoring their own recent history, Democrats said that nothing could be more un-American than to root for Obama to fail. Of course, they did not consider it un-American when Obama, during his time in the Senate, joined Senate Majority Leader Harry Reid and then Speaker of the House Nancy Pelosi in openly declaring that the U.S. had failed in the Global War on Terrorism, undermining United States military efforts in an attempt to get back into power. In February 2007, Obama stated that the lives of American soldiers had been "wasted" on the war in Iraq.[1] Earlier he had proposed a bill in the Senate to withdraw combat troops by the end of March of 2008, which would have relegated the highly successful "Surge" ineffective. That led then Australian Prime Minister John Howard to issue this stinging rebuke of Obama's plan: "If I were running Al Qaeda in Iraq, I would put a circle around March 2008 and pray as many times as possible for a victory not only for Obama, but also for the Democrats."

In April 2007, Reid declared, "This war is lost and the surge is not accomplishing anything"; and Pelosi announced to the world that we had lost in Iraq and we should bring the troops home in defeat, empowering our enemies to kill more American soldiers just as the Troop Surge was getting underway.[2] And they did it for selfish reasons: undermining the war effort with abject lies and dividing the nation provided them an opportunity to win more seats in congress and, the following year, the White House. Undermining the U.S. military is far more un-American than anything anyone has said about Obama, and it has inspired more ferocity from our enemy which led to the death of more American soldiers. On April 23, 2007, nine members of the 82nd Airborne Division were killed in a truck bomb explosion that left 20 others wounded. An Al Qaida front group in Iraq claimed credit for the attack.

It was bad enough that Democrats and "journalists" were labeling the war as a military loss, but they were also insisting that Republicans agree with them. But Operation Iraqi Freedom was not a military loss at all. We annihilated the Iraqi Army, put the leader of the country in jail, and his entire leadership structure was either killed or sent into hiding. The initial Iraq war was over within months of the invasion. Yet, it continued to rage here in the U.S. with Democrats and their allies in the liberal media insisting that the U.S. military was defeated. The enemy didn't even think they had won until they noticed that American journalists and power-seeking politicians were dumb enough to claim that America had lost the war. Only then did they too begin to crow that the U.S. had been defeated. The U.S. military performed extraordinarily well in the invasion and occupation. The residual criticism was that we weren't refereeing the sectarian disputes very well; but what does that have to do with a military victory? The liberal claim that we lost the war in Iraq because Muslims were killing each other while the freely elected Iraqi authorities were showing little initiative to stop them is preposterous.

The Islamic extremists the U.S. routed so severely in Iraq must have been shocked to read in U.S. newspapers that they had somehow won the war. I am sure they were initially hesitant to accept the victory, figuring it must be a trick of some sort because no one could be so stupid. However, eventually the *New York Times* convinced them that instead of hiding from us, they should

5

be taking a propaganda victory lap, which they did and surely thought Stalin a genius, "Useful idiots indeed!"

When Democrats undermine national security, dissent is patriotic; when conservatives tell the truth about Democrats, it's "un-American." The Democrats and media who pretended to misunderstand Limbaugh's comment knew what conservatives suspected about Obama: that he did not believe in American Exceptionalism, saw no value in the U.S. Constitution limiting the powers of the federal government, and would seek to change the Constitution, not through legal means, but through executive fiat. In short, liberals knew the intended meaning of Limbaugh's remark: in order for the Republic to survive, Obama has to fail in his plans to "fundamentally transform" the U.S. government and executive power. Not that this understanding prevented them from seizing on Limbaugh's imperfect phrasing to attack all conservatives.

What is striking about all this is that while Obama has declared war on his fellow Americans and our way of life for merely disagreeing with him on policy and governance, he has attempted to establish friendly relations with some of the worst people in the world: anti-American dictators and self-proclaimed enemies of the United States. Perhaps voters should have noticed when so many of our nations' enemies were supporting Obama during the presidential campaign. Hamas leaders endorsed him, as did Iranian dictator Mahmoud Ahmadinejad, Cuban fascist Fidel Castro, and Venezuelan strongman Hugo Chavez. Obama continues to impress the enemies of America, in 2012 he earned the confidence and picked up an endorsement from the corrupt leadership of Russia. Obama advocated patient negotiation with the Iranian despot and the terrorist group Hamas, while savaging patriotic Americans who have policy disagreements with him. So, it appears Obama is friendlier to those who hate America than he is to those who love it. Obama has given the enemies of America plenty of reasons to love him.

In 2009, one day after his inauguration, the Associated Press ran an article with the headline "Open Government Advocates Praise Obama Move on Disclosure." The lead was, "Government watchdogs are cheering President Barack Obama's move to change how open records laws are interpreted as a sign of greater disclosure of agency information than during the Bush administration."[3]

The article explains, "In the late 1970s, Carter's attorney general, Griffin Bell, issued guidance to err on the side of releasing information. Under Reagan, William French Smith came in and reversed that; he told them, 'when in doubt withhold.' Then under Clinton, Janet Reno reversed it again; she told agencies their presumption should be for release."[4]

Is that so? I don't remember the Clinton administration's openness that way at all. In fact, I am still waiting for documents to come back from Freedom of Information Act requests that I filed as a journalist back in 1995, 1996, 1997, and 1998.

The Clinton White House was sued multiple times for withholding information that had nothing to do with national security. At one point, a federal judge held the Clintons in contempt for not producing information about their healthcare taskforce that Hillary Clinton had established in secret for what was to become the failed "Hillarycare" proposal. I guess they didn't get Reno's memo about openness. Or perhaps they just didn't want enemies of America to know how to sign up for the free healthcare.

Throughout the Clinton years, congressional oversight committee investigations were frequently frustrated by the Clintons' failure to turn over information so those committees could fulfill their legal obligation to the Constitution. And what about Reno herself? She steadfastly refused to release what became known as "the Freeh, LaBella Memo" about the Department of Justice investigation of Clinton's Chinese campaign fundraising scandal. I guess the reason I remember these things is because I actually covered them at the time, while the Associated Press was busy digging for dirt on the Republicans in Congress who were requesting those Clinton documents.

But now as we were told, "The fact that Mr. Obama took these actions on his very first day in office signals a new era in government accountability."[5] Well, how about that. The man who ran for president without revealing even the most basic information about his personal background announced to the media that he would throw open our government for everyone to inspect.

To be clear, the openness the media and Democrats are celebrating have nothing to do with how the government is squandering tax money, transparency of bailout funds, or Obama's White House scandals. No, the transparency that we are now supposed to celebrate is over national security secrets. That is, how the Bush administration conducted the war on terrorism. This is Shangri-La for Democrats—and terrorists. Having our game plan for the war on terror being laid out wide-open for the Left and the enemy to openly criticize and dissect (and thereby weaken) makes it much easier for our enemies to plan another attack on America.

Where was all of the media's concern with openness during Obama's campaign? Obama ran for the highest office in the land with the shortest list of accomplishments in history. It should have been easy to uncover everything about him; yet, somehow, we still know nothing. Obama's medical records have never been released. We know only from an admission in his first autobiography that he was a recreational drug user.

We know nothing about his academic record at Columbia or Harvard except the piece he wants us to know: that he held a senior position at the Harvard Law Review. Why can't we see the academic record that earned him that spot?

In 2008, journalist Kenneth Timmerman reported highly intriguing details of how Obama got accepted into Harvard Law School and how tuition may have been paid. Timmerman's multiple reports on the subject detailed intentional deception by the Obama campaign, cover up, a Muslim extremist with connections to the Saudi royal family, and no evidence whatsoever to back up the story Obama was telling the press. At the time, I queried several reporters covering the Obama campaign as to why they weren't investigating these allegations and did not receive an adequate response from any of them.

During the campaign, the *National Review* complained that Obama refused, for no apparent reason, to release the names of his law clients. Instead, Obama chose to release his firm's entire client list, thus avoiding any scrutiny of possible conflicts of interest. We still don't know precisely what his relationship is to the controversial group ACORN, or to unrepentant terrorist William Ayers (even though he clearly has relationships with both) and no one from the media has pressed him for details. Ayers, for example, claimed that he wrote Obama's first book, Dreams from My Father, which still merits inquiry, especially since Obama has boasted that he wrote both of his books himself.

This is just a short list of things we don't know about Obama. Indeed, the unanswered questions indicate that there is much more that voters should have known before the 2008 election. Four years later all of those questions still linger.

Just three months after assuming office, Obama released CIA interrogation memos of terrorist detainees to the press with resounding cheers from the media, liberals and Al Qaida. The *New York Times* gleefully reported them, to the detriment of our national security: "The techniques were among the Bush administration's most closely guarded secrets, and the documents released Thursday afternoon were the most comprehensive public accounting to date of the program."[6]

Democrats and the media tell us it is a cause for celebration that we have opened up our national security secrets for the world, including hostile foreign powers, to see. But more than five years after Obama declared his run for the presidency we still know very little about the man to whom we have handed the keys to the kingdom. Bush kept interrogation techniques under wraps because exposing them would make our country more vulnerable. What is Obama's excuse?

Chapter 2

Tinker, Tailor, Soldier, President

British Cold War spy novelist John LeCarre could draw enough inspiration for an entirely new series of post Cold War non-fiction from Obama's relationship with Moscow. Obama's Russia policy seems not to be based on leftist Cold War ideology, but on the nonsensical revisionist concept that the United States lost the war altogether and thereby must genuflect to the corrupt Russian leadership.

In a scene that can only be described as bizarre and chilling, Obama was making a few final private remarks to Russian President Dmitry Medvedev at the end of a summit when, unbeknownst to Obama, the microphones of reporters present at the meeting were able to give Americans a glimpse of the sheer cynicism and dastardliness of President Obama.

Obama: "On all these issues, but particularly missile defense, this, this can be solved but it's important for him [Vladimir Putin] to give me space."

President Medvedev: "Yeah, I understand. I understand your message about space. Space for you…"

President Obama: "This is my last election. After my election I have more flexibility."

President Medvedev: "I understand. I will transmit this information to Vladimir."

What an ominous forecast. That an American president would tell the leader of another country that he needed "space" to mislead his own citizens in order to be reelected so he can then create policy that favors that leader's country is scandalous enough, but this was not even the first time Obama had taken drastic steps to help Russia at the expense of American national security interests and those of our true allies.

A year and a half before the surreptitiously taped conversation between Obama and the Russian premier, Medvedev awarded Russia's highest honor to ten spies that had penetrated the U.S. In late June 2010, the FBI captured the ten Russians, who had been living and working here for at least ten years under deep cover as part of a sleeper cell. These agents established contacts with both Obama officials and Clinton officials. According to the *Washington Post*, "'Their mission was to gather information and identify potential future government employees who could be helpful,' officials said."[7]

Little did they know, Obama would eventually prove to be shockingly helpful on his own. Other reports said the spies were tasked to gather information about what possible negotiating positions the administration might have regarding treaties and arms control agreements. Obama made it clear that Russia didn't need spies for that, under his "reset" policy he would just whisper to Medvedev that as long as he could feign toughness to get reelected he would be extremely flexible regarding missile defense.

Usually, captured spies face years in prison and intense interrogation in an effort to discover exactly what the infiltrators know, who they answer to in their own country, and who they have been in contact with inside the U.S. —the type of information that is vital to national security. But that didn't happen in this case. Writing in the *Wall Street Journal*, former head of U.S. Counterintelligence, Michelle Van Cleave expressed concern over Obama's reaction to such devastating penetration: "In 2010, the

FBI rolled up 10 'illegals' – all Russian citizens living here under deep cover, part of a clandestine espionage support network under tightly held investigation for over a decade. Their long-awaited in-custody interviews promised rare insights into Russian intelligence operations in this country. Instead, all 10 were sent off to Moscow in a pre-emptive 'spy swap' before they could even get debriefed."[8]

In less than two weeks after being caught, these deep pene-trating moles were whisked off to a hero's welcome back in Moscow. Eric Holder's Justice Department immediately returned them to Russia before our counter-intelligence agencies could interrogate these spies, thereby undermining a criminal case, which a federal court in Manhattan was planning to bring against them. Because of this act, investigators will never know the true extent to which these Russian agents were able to carry out their mission of infiltrating policymaking circles in Washington and New York to collect intelligence on the state of American politics and foreign policy to guide Russian relations with the U.S. We will also never know how effective the Russians were in recruiting Americans inside the U.S. government into their espionage ring.

This whole deal smelled so bad that even the *Washington Post* had to acknowledge it: "John L. Martin, who supervised dozens of espionage cases during a 26-year career at the Justice Depart-ment, said earlier spy exchanges took years to work out. The speed at which the latest one occurred was 'absolutely unprece-dented,' he said."[9]

The *Post* also recognized the severity of Obama's actions re-garding the case by summing it up in political terms referring to the swap of ten freshly apprehended covert agents for four Russians, some of whom were merely accused of illegal contacts with Americans, and had been in Russian jails for years: "Indeed, the swap could feed Republican criticism that the Obama administration is too accommodating toward Russia."[10]

"Accommodating toward Russia?" This was much more than "accommodating." The Obama Administration approached Russia on bended knee. It was almost as though the United States had done something wrong by rounding up their spies in our country. According to the *Post* article: "Obama administration officials said the deal illustrated the good working relationship between the former Cold War enemies. After initially denying that the agents worked for Moscow, the Russian government did an about-face and was willing to deal, U.S. officials said."[11]

The Russians plant deep moles into the U.S. and after we catch them in the act of spying, we immediately return them, without serious interrogation, and this administration calls that a "good working relationship?" I would hate to see what Obama considers appeasement.

The *Post* also reveals an almost delusional view from Obama insiders about the spy swap: "'We drove the terms of this arrangement, which was based on national security as well as humanitarian grounds,' said one of the U.S. officials."[12]

Sure. Obama forced the Russians to accept this deal. The same way lottery winners are forced to cash their checks. According to the *Post*: "The quick agreement suggested both Washington and Moscow wanted to move beyond the scandal, which occurred as the Senate is weighing a new bilateral nuclear arms-control accord."[13]

It makes perfect sense why Moscow would want to sweep this under the rug; but why would the U.S. have any interest in protecting the reputation of a country caught spying on us? Unless, of course, Obama was planning to hand Moscow everything it desires with regards to American unilateral disarmament. In that case, Obama wouldn't want the American people to dwell on the fact that Russia is treating us like their Cold War adversary and we are treating them as an ally.

Several months later, immediately following the 2010 elections where Republicans gained seats in the Senate, Obama rushed the New START Treaty through the lame-duck Senate in a manner that was legally dubious at best. The Senate quickly ratified this treaty with "no changes," per the demands of the Russian government. Like its predecessor, New START heavily favored Russia's national security at great cost to ours by including no provisions for Russian disarmament of its tactical nuclear weapons, where Russia has a significant advantage over the U.S.

The excuses for Obama to push through the New START were pathetic. Basically those in favor insist that the treaty would allow U.S. inspectors back into Russia to make sure the Russians are eliminating their nuclear stockpile in accordance with the treaty. Mitigating that, however, is the fact that our inspectors can only look at the sites that the Russians tell us we can inspect. That's it. That's the best argument Obama had for supporting the treaty. On the other hand, you could write a thicker book than this about the reasons to reject it.

Russia desperately wanted the U.S. to sign this treaty. In fact, Russian leaders even warned us that we had better not tamper with the language of the treaty while it was being considered during the lame-duck (illegitimate) Senate session. One of the reasons they couldn't contain their participatory enthusiasm is that the treaty limits our ability to deploy a missile defense system. And we just might need that missile defense system because the treaty calls for reductions in our arsenal of nuclear-armed missiles, which puts Russia at an even greater strategic offensive advantage.

It is complicated to explain, but to simplify the effect of the New START treaty, imagine that the U.S. has a handgun and five bullets, and the Russians have a handgun and ten bullets. Russian Premier Medvedev says to Obama that he will throw away five of his bullets if Obama throws away five of his. Only an idiot would take that deal. Well, an idiot or someone who doesn't mind selling out his country.

But there is a precedent to this stupidity. In 1998, the Russians made the outlandish argument that the 1972 Anti-Ballistic Missile Treaty did not apply to them because they were no longer the USSR, but it did apply to us because we were still the United States. Communist China, which was never involved in the ABM Treaty, also asserted that the U.S. should be bound by it. Most observers at the time were sure the Russians and Chinese were "punking" us, but it ended up not being a joke, and furthermore, President Clinton somehow agreed with them. In short, Clinton sided with the two most dangerous countries on the planet at that time, against his own country. No wonder many senior people who worked in national security in the nineties were quietly saying Clinton was a traitor. (I am not kidding.)

So why would any Republican vote to ratify such a treaty? Who knows? Fourteen of them did, even though they could have defeated it because treaties require a two-thirds vote for passage. Instead they allowed the lame-duck passage even knowing that it would have been likely to fail during the next legitimate session because of the increased number of new conservative Republican Senators. But they did it anyway, and one thing we know for sure is that when it is revealed that the world is more dangerous because of this treaty, the Democrats will remind us that Republicans voted to ratify it, too, making it historically "bipartisan."

The Russians, and their previous incarnation the Soviet Union, were notorious for not abiding by any of these agreements they signed with the United States. In fact, at the very moment the Obama Administration was bum-rushing this treaty through the Senate, the Russians had already been refusing to comply with another agreement, the Treaty on Conventional Armed Forces in Europe (CFE). The CFE treaty was signed in 1990 and was intended to "establish military parity and stability in the conventional military forces and equipment of Europe between the NATO countries and those of the Warsaw bloc." According to an *Agence France Presse* report, "Russia suspended its observance of the treaty in 2007" while the U.S. continued to meet its obligations under the treaty for four years before the State Department began, reluctantly, to reconsider unilateral adherence to the treaty.[14]

In 2009, while Russia was failing to comply with the CFE treaty, Obama sold out our allies, Poland and the Czech Republic, by announcing that we were pulling out our missile defense systems from those two countries, a drastic move that Moscow had demanded the Obama administration take. The Bush administration had developed the system and provided for its deployment in the two eastern European allies who were once members of the Soviet Bloc, ostensibly to defend against long range Iranian missiles. But the Poles and Czechs saw the defense system and the strategic relationship with the U.S. as insurance against Russia's nostalgia for its hegemony in the region. And with good reason—only months earlier Russia had invaded Georgia and was at the time fighting for increased control in Ukraine. This announcement came despite the fact that the two countries had welcomed the presence of those systems, which we had promised to build in response to Iran's recent testing of a ballistic missile that could reach Poland.

The Czechs and the Poles acknowledged that they had been sold out by Obama. *Fox News* reported on the reaction from Poland, "Polish President Lech Kaczynski said he was concerned that Obama's new strategy leaves Poland in a dangerous 'gray zone' between Western Europe and the old Soviet sphere." A similar reaction came from the Czech Republic according to the *Fox News* report, "An editorial in Hospodarske Novine, a respected pro-business Czech newspaper, said: 'An ally we rely on has betrayed us, and exchanged us for its own, better relations with Russia, of which we are rightly afraid.'"[15]

It was bad enough that Obama caved to Russia's demands and abandoned two staunch U.S. allies, but he did it on the 70th anniversary of the Soviet invasion of Poland, as if to celebrate the reemergence of Russia to its position of dominance over these now free and democratic nations.

In light of Obama's apparent strategy of allowing Russia to think they won the Cold War, it should come as no surprise that he plans to hand over top-secret weapons technology. In January 2012, the *Washington Times* reported Obama's intentions in his signing statement attached to the 2012 defense authorization bill, "Mr. Obama said restrictions aimed at protecting top-secret technical data on U.S. Standard Missile-3 velocity burnout parameters might impinge on his constitutional foreign policy authority."[16]

An earlier *Washington Times* report stated that "U.S. officials are planning to provide Moscow with the SM-3 data, despite reservations from security officials who say that doing so could compromise the effectiveness of the system by allowing Russian weapons technicians to counter the missile. The weapons are considered some of the most effective high-speed interceptors in the U.S. missile defense arsenal."[17]

So not only did Obama remove our missile defense system from our allies Poland and the Czech Republic, he has now told Russia exactly how to attack not only those allies, but America itself.

For anyone who doubts the damage Obama has done to America's national security or how it will make the entire free world less safe in the future, just look at what is happening on the Korean Peninsula right now. North Korea has nuclear weapons today because of the Clinton administration's 1994 "Agreed Framework," a fool's bargain that was supposed to ensure that North Korea did not get nuclear weapons. But instead of preventing them from getting nukes, it managed to accelerate their nuclear program. Throughout the rest of the Clinton years, career intelligence analysts were advising them in no uncertain terms that North Korea was cheating on the agreement and pursuing nukes more rapidly with technology we provided them under terms of the agreement. But, instead of acknowledging the failure of the "Agreed Framework" and fixing it, Clinton and his people crowed about its success in stopping the dangerous Kim Jong Ill from getting the very bomb that his son, Kim Jong Un threatens the Pacific Rim with now. Duplicitous Democrats such as Clinton and Obama cannot be trusted to negotiate sensitive national security agreements.

Obama's words and actions in his dealings with Russia have been dangerous and, at times, borderline treasonous. In his own words to Russian President Medvedev, he revealed that his reelection would usher in new U.S. policies under which Russia would be allowed to strengthen its military capabilities at the direct expense of U.S. national defense. He all but said, "I am only pretending to be looking after my own country." And regardless of his intentions for our national security, Obama's acknowledgement that he could not be honest about his intentions in an election year drives home the additional point that he does not want Americans to go to the polls with accurate information about his plans to placate Russia. We as a nation have allowed our national defense to be greatly undermined by left-wing presidents like Obama and Clinton, and aided by liberals in Congress who are hell-bent on redistributing America's military advantage to the rest of the world. At the core of their actions seems to be the bizarre belief that the U.S. lacks the moral authority to be the world's lone superpower. Apparently, they believe the nations that are actively spying on us are more worthy of being trusted with our own defense technology than we are.

Chapter 3

Courier to Peking

Barack Obama is not the first American president to undermine the security of his country. Bill Clinton, in many ways, was even worse. Clinton started the national security decline of the U.S. and did far more damage than even Wiki leaks founder Julian Assange, a character with whom Clinton shares eerie similarities.

Both project notably anti-American attitudes. Both exposed U.S. national security secrets to the international community. And both were undone by claims of sexual harassment. Unfortunately neither was ever charged appropriately for the subversive activities in which they routinely engaged. And the similarities don't end there. Both are self-aggrandizing, needy narcissists who require power in order to bed women. And both betrayed Hillary Clinton.

Odious though he may be, based on what we know of Assange, he at least has a better case to defend his actions than Clinton. After all, Assange is Australian, so he didn't sell out his own country the way Clinton did by spilling the secrets of the United States. And while Assange made the secrets he stole available to the entire world, Clinton sent them directly to Communist China.

America's Left (including the media) would prefer that Americans not be reminded of what Clinton did in the 90s. In fact, most of the media virtually ignored one of the biggest scandals of our nation's history. In 1992, Bill Clinton won the presidency, in part by criticizing George H. W. Bush for coddling "the butchers of Beijing." Then, immediately upon assuming office, he began to decontrol weapons technology to these very butchers. That technology propelled China's weapon production through the next eight years at near-warp speed, transforming their "junk-yard army" of 1992 into one of the most technologically advanced war-machines on the planet. They built this machine to be capable, in their own words, of "controlling the initiative" in the "inevitable" war with the United States. Just a partial list of the things Clinton elected to donate the Chinese military enterprise: cryptographic technology, ballistic missile technology, nuclear weapons technology, and technologies detailing how to strike several American cities with multiple warheads carried on one missile.

While Bill Clinton was aiding the Communist Chinese military, he was simultaneously receiving millions of dollars in illegal donations from Chinese nationals. All of this is documented in reports from congressional investigations at the time. Essential elements of those investigations will remain sealed for many decades. Republicans, who then had the authority to make this information public, decided it would be better for America if the rest of the world didn't know the extent of President Clinton's corruption. And while it's nice that someone was concerned with defending America's position in the world, it's that logic that ensures the Communist Chinese alone know the extent to which they compromised Clinton. The American people, for whom Clinton ostensibly worked, and whose blood will be shed whenever China decides to take "initiative," have been denied the opportunity to hold the man responsible.

So, Clinton managed to skate by without completely trashing his reputation. Assange, on the other hand, is technologically crafty, but totally devoid of political savvy. When leaking documents merely endangered American soldiers, sailors and airmen, the liberal media and the Obama administration raised little objection to him. For example, in July 2010, *ABC News' Nightline* broadcast featured reporter Jim Sciutto promoting Assange's allegations against American troops in Afghanistan. In a story that opened with "Most alarmingly, they contain what critics claim is evidence of possible war crimes by U.S. soldiers. Well, we sat down with the man behind the leak, Julian Assange." Nightline portrayed Assange as a concerned citizen of the world. Up until November of 2010, Assange's leaks were damaging to the Bush administration and the U.S. military, and thus perfectly palatable for the liberal media to report. But then Assange made a devastating tactical error, from a political standpoint anyway. Assange foolishly released documents embarrassing to the Obama administration. And then he did the unthinkable: He demanded that Hillary Clinton be fired. The Democrat and mainstream media love affair with Assange turned out to be a one-night-stand. Now he had crossed the line. A couple of weeks later he was picked up on the charge of using a bad condom, thus solidifying his fraternity with Bill Clinton. Clearly at that point, the uniformed Democrats (and covert Democrats in the media) were truly steamed. The media didn't even object when Assange was denied bail for the seemingly insignificant charge for which he was arrested. Stay tuned for their embrace of extraordinary rendition... and perhaps even Assange's permanent relocation to Abu Ghraib or Guantanamo Bay since he had now crossed la noblesse.

Since his departure from the White House, Clinton has tried obsessively to resurrect his image. He's been dogged, and he has been successful. Abetted by the so-called mainstream media, who continue to ignore the direct correlation between Communist China's powerful new military and the weapons technology transferred to them by Clinton, he has honed his "legacy-building" to an art form. Even some who claim to be in the "conservative media" have assisted Clinton in this process, ingratiating themselves with puff pieces. Note to Assange: if you have the Clinton/China documents Republicans won't let us see, please leak them at once; at the very least, it might get some momentum behind your demand that Hillary be fired.

It was the eight years of Clinton that led to a disgraceful spectacle in the White House under Obama. January 17, 2011 there was jubilation throughout Beijing among Communist Party officials as President Hu Jintao was greeted by Obama with a lavish reception and the first state dinner for a Chinese official since Clinton was president. According to the *Epoch Times*, a global newspaper with an emphasis on Communist China, the musical guest performing at the gala, a pianist named Lang Lang, played a song widely known in China as an anti-American anthem. It is the theme song of a very famous Chinese movie.

"The film depicts a group of 'People's Volunteer Army' soldiers who are first hemmed in at Shanganling (or Triangle Hill) and then, when reinforcements arrive, take up their rifles and counterattack the U.S. military 'jackals'," stated the *Epoch Times*.[18]

According to reports, millions of Chinese watched Lang's performance on the Internet after being told in advance about the planned insult. Hu was celebrating the Communist Chinese growing influence over the U.S. Unfortunately for the peasants of China it meant that they could no longer see the U.S. as a beacon of freedom and hope. America was now honoring their oppressors; it must have been a time of great sadness for them, just as it was for the Americans that were aware of the insult.

Coincidently, I am sure, just before Hu's visit, the Chinese unveiled their new J-20 stealth fighter. They're boasting that it is a great feat of engineering. It is really stolen pieces of American ingenuity and brilliance cobbled together into a sort of chop shop fighter plane.

In March of 1999, an American F-117 stealth fighter was lost when Serbs shot it down over Yugoslavia during what Serbs call "Monica's War" due to the curious timing that coincided with the Clinton/Lewinsky investigation. At the time there were reports that China was there gathering parts from the downed plane. Whatever the Chinese collected from that scavenger hunt simply sped up the development process for what they had already bought or stolen directly from the United States.

The Chinese obtained stealth capabilities from substances that used to be mined and processed exclusively in the United States, where the manufacturing processes was closely guarded. That is, until the Clinton administration shut down mines rich in exotic materials crucial to the development of high-tech weapons technology. Clinton then allowed Communist Chinese front companies to walk in and buy the entire means of production— even as they were producing critical parts for our most closely protected weapons systems—and ship those weapons factories to China. Career national security analysts warned the Clinton administration at the time of the dire consequences of allowing these technologies and manufacturing tools to leave the United States. Those analysts were harassed, threatened and fired for simply doing their job—protecting American national security.

It's likely that parts of the J-20's wings are made of a miraculous substance invented in a naval ordnance laboratory where a Chinese spy posing as a student stole it. That substance will increase the maneuverability of China's J-20, thereby increasing its effectiveness when doing battle with American fighter pilots and in strafing runs at soldiers, or as they like to call us, "jackals." Other technology that Clinton allowed the Chinese to steal or buy gave the Communist government a technological advantage which they used to further oppress their own citizens. And the liberal Democrats, if not running defense for Clinton, were curiously silent after they, including Clinton himself, chastised the first President Bush for being soft on China and failing to do enough to stop the many human rights violations committed in that nation.

At the time of Hu's visit, media pundits and former State Department flacks insisted that it would be bad for President Obama to bring up China's human rights record in public because it would embarrass President Hu. Those issues, we are told, are best discussed behind closed doors. Not everyone on the Left agrees though. A story in the *Washington Post* from January 2011, quotes Tom Malinowski, the Washington director of Human Rights Watch, as saying "it's important for Obama to 'lay down a marker' in his conversations with Hu" about how Chinese leaders oppress their own citizens.[19] Whatever stealth markers Obama may have lain down are meaningless because he, like Clinton before him, has done so much to weaken his own country that such warnings are no longer credible. It is safe to conclude, then, that Hu is less likely to heed Obama's suggestions on how to improve his country's dismal human rights record than he is to thank the United States for providing China's military with the technology responsible for its recent meteoric rise to prominence.

So in the end, while our leaders tried desperately to avoid offending Hu, the Chinese premier held a victory celebration in the White House. Obama sat through the entertainment, staring down his nose at the spectacle as though the entertainers were court minstrels performing for his pleasure; apparently oblivious to the fact that they were flagrantly mocking and ridiculing him in the castle he borrowed from the American people.

Chapter 4

Winning the Hearts and Wallets of Terrorists

As lies and corruption began bleeding through a fading façade of "hope and change," many Americans began to fear that they had been duped into voting for a pig in a poke, and Obama's approval rating started to show it. By the second week in March of Obama's first year in office, the difference between those who strongly approved of Obama and those who strongly disapproved had shrunk to single digits according to the very reliable Rasmussen Polling Firm. But despite the domestic dissention, Obama remained very popular among one of his key foreign constituencies—terrorists.

The terrorist group Hamas endorsed Obama in 2008, but instead of feeling suckered like many of the Americans who voted for him, they have actually seen results. An *Agence France Presse* report from March of 2009 quoted Hamas leader Khaled Meshaal praising what he calls Obama's "new lexicon" for describing terrorist's demands. "The challenge for everyone is that [Obama's new language] is a prelude to a sincere change in U.S. . . . foreign policy," said Meshaal.[20]

By "sincere change" the Hamas leader was referring to the previous U.S. policy in the Middle East that stated unequivocally that we would not support Hamas' goal of killing all the Jews, taking over Israeli land and turning it into the new Palestine. That is the reason for Hamas' existence. There is no arguing this point: it is stated clearly in Hamas' charter, has been reiterated constantly ever since, and rewritten in the blood of over eight hundred Jews they have murdered since organization was founded in 1988.

Obama is reaching out a friendly hand to the terrorist organization that has not only murdered hundreds of innocent Israeli women and children, but plenty of Americans as well. Hamas has also threatened attacks within the United States several times and has had its agents interdicted while attempting to carry out these threats. Ironically, it was the same Israelis Obama seeks to abandon who tipped us off to those planned attacks.

While Obama has repeatedly sought to embrace every anti-American entity that would listen to him, he has shown no such respect to our country's allies. Within days of taking office, he insulted Great Britain, an ally that showed tremendous support in the war on terror, by sending back a bust of Winston Churchill. This piece was a gift from the British shortly after the September 11 attacks to symbolize that the United Kingdom would stand with the U.S. through the uncertain and trying times that were to follow. The British were deeply offended by Obama's insult and many felt it foreshadowed Obama's plan of imposing his anti-American worldview on our nation and her allies.

Americans should hope that America's allies don't read too much into Obama's first term foreign policy strategy, because if he gets a second term they might start attacking us just to curry favor with the administration.

During the Bush administration, when the French opposed our war effort in Iraq, Democrats demanded that the leadership in Paris approve our national security policy. Once Obama discovered that France had elected an anti-terrorist and pro-American leader, Nicholas Sarkozy, Obama and the Democrats immediately abandoned their interest in getting French advice on

U.S. national security and placed them among the rest of our allies on Obama's watch list.

Obama has elevated the most dangerous regimes in the world, such as Iran, to worthy negotiating partners and terrorists groups such as Hamas (which controls Gaza), and the Muslim Brotherhood (now running Egypt), to future rogue-nation leaders. "As I said in my inauguration speech, if countries like Iran are willing to unclench their fist, they will find an extended hand from us," Obama said in an interview with Al-Arabiya shortly after assuming office.[21] The world was a dangerous place in 2008 and four years of President Obama has made it even worse—especially for the U.S. and Israel.

In June 2009, Obama rewarded Hamas with a visit from former President Jimmy Carter who became the highest-ranking official to ever meet with Hamas. Carter stated that he was there as a "private citizen," but was preparing a report for the Obama administration about the visit. Hamas exploited the occasion to use Carter as public relations flak for the truly gullible. A lot comes to mind when trying to characterize Carter's periodic misadventures in the Middle East, but two phrases keep recurring: a basket case of self-delusion and venal anti-Semitism masquerading as compassion. In either case, Carter is relentless in his support of the outlawed terrorist organization Hamas to pursue its murderous policies aimed primarily at civilians.

During his foray into Gaza—where Carter publicly called upon the U.S. to remove the Iranian-backed, Muslim Brotherhood-affiliated Hamas from the list of known terrorist organizations—he managed to be the only observer of Mid-East politics to believe the absolutely phony and poorly staged "falling out" between Hamas leader Khaled Mashaal and his deputy Moussa Abu Marzook. What Carter interpreted as a sign of Hamas's moderation was, in fact, a clumsy tactical move to make that organization appear "moderate" by spinning off its terrorist operational arm into a subsidiary organization so that when the next series of terror attacks occur, they will have a degree of deniability for the actions they launch. This is an old tactic taken directly from the terrorist playbook of the late Yassir Arafat. It also came at a time when Obama was attempting to legitimize Hamas and preparing to send them financial aid. In fact, some reports indicated that Carter was delivering that message from Obama.

Since Carter seemed like a willing audience for their clumsy theatrics, there was also a staged "roadside bomb" incident where Hamas announced they had discovered and neutralized a bomb along Carter's motorcade route. Of course he was deeply grateful for their vigilance, professionalism, and concern for his safety. Again, he stood alone in his gullibility. Virtually all observers of the trip were convinced that Hamas planted the "bomb" themselves, and then rode in as heroes to daringly disarm it. Such feeble play-acting can be a slick political strategy, as long as you are dealing with Jimmy Carter.

While in Gaza, Carter also urged Hamas to recognize the right of Israel to exist. Can we now get Carter to urge Obama to recognize Israel's right to exist? Exposing the uselessness of this entire gambit, a senior Hamas official announced: "Recognizing Israel is completely unacceptable." Undaunted by the obvious facts concerning the violent and implacable nature of his Hamas friends, Carter is still insists that U.S. and UN sanctions against Hamas be lifted and they be rewarded for their vile rejectionist stance—after all, the people in Gaza who freely elected them are suffering under their policies. Shockingly, Carter's favorite terrorist organization actually goes through with what they say they believe in.

Unfortunately, multitudes of innocent people pay the ultimate price for the delusional machinations of such self-righteous weaklings who periodically appear on the world stage. During his failed one-term presidency, Carter was largely responsible for the mismanagement of regime change in Iran that saw Muslim fundamentalists seize power in 1979. His intervention to forestall a military coup ensured the successful power grab by Islamic militants and the ensuing waves of assassinations of pro-Western Iranian leaders around the world. These same Islamic militants went on to seize control of the American Embassy, and develop terrorism as their primary instrument of foreign policy by creating Hezbollah, a terrorist group second only to al Qaeda in American deaths.

There is a certain symmetry to Carter's unwavering support for organizations like Hamas. How much is a result of his underlying guilt as the unwitting mid-wife of modern day Islamic terrorism and how much is sheer buffoonery is difficult to discern. Unfortunately, his misplaced compassion for Hamas and the Gazans who put them in power and continue to support them despite the depredations they have wrought may also mask a long-suspected, unspoken anti-Semitism that distorts his ability to rationally approach issues in the Middle-East.

Neville Chamberlain saw the world as he wished it would be in 1938 when he signed the Munich Agreement with Hitler and doomed the innocent citizens of Czechoslovakia, and eventually much of Europe, to Nazi tyranny and genocide. He lived to see his 76th birthday. Jimmy Carter has now seen his 86th birthday, but his legitimization of terrorist organizations such as Hamas will ensure that untold numbers of innocent civilians will never be blessed with such longevity.

June of 2010, one year after Carter's visit to Gaza, President Obama transformed the United States, both technically and literally, into a "state sponsor of terrorism," a designation that, when applied to other countries, means no aid, no trade, and such a nation is an adversary of the U.S. and her allies. Like many of the ambiguities chasing Obama, his announcement of a $400 million aid package to the West Bank and Gaza, stunned anyone who understands the region. The West Bank and Gaza were at the time, and still are, two separate entities; the West Bank under the control of Mahmoud Abbas, reputed to be a moderate by radical Islamic standards, and Gaza, which is run by the democratically-elected Islamic Resistance Movement, better known as Hamas.

When announcing this "aid package" to Gaza, Obama must have thought us a nation of fools. Who can blame him? After all, we elected him president without knowing anything about him. Abbas is not the head of Gaza. Perhaps it was a parlor trick to have Abbas physically present at the White House when Obama made the announcement, as if it would somehow con-flate – in the collective mind of the media – Abbas, who they accept as a moderate, and the radical terrorist group Hamas into one acceptably moderate amalgam. However you characterize the charade, it was clearly a bold attempt to avoid scrutiny while handing over American tax dollars to a terrorist organization that has murdered American citizens.

Whatever else you can say about Obama, at least he never forgets his friends. Thanks to the dogged investigative journalism of Aaron Klein, we know that some Gazans bought themselves a stake in the Obama presidency. "Palestinian brothers inside the

Hamas-controlled Gaza Strip are listed in government election filings as having donated $29,521.54 to Sen. Barack Obama's campaign," Klein reported in 2008. Perhaps the Palestinians and Hamas knew more about Obama than we did. Of course, no one else in the media cared much where Obama got his campaign money, even though contributions like this were illegal for multiple reasons.

The timing of Obama's announcement was rather curious. Late May 2010, Israel had just taken action against ships that were calling themselves a "freedom flotilla," sponsored by the Free Gaza movement. The ships were attempting to break Israel's blockade of Gaza, put in place specifically to stop the flow of weapons and war supplies that Hamas uses to attack Israel and its citizens. Israeli soldiers boarded the ship and were violently attacked by the so-called "peace activists." The soldiers responded in kind by dispatching the attackers. Obama rushed to join the rest of the Islamic world in condemning Israel for taking action to defend itself against this violation of its sovereign waters. "Gaza has become the symbol in the Arab world of the Israeli treatment of Palestinians, and we have to change that," said an unnamed White House official to the *New York Times* following the incident.[22] Secretary of State Hillary Clinton demanded an investigation of Israel's actions in defending itself. A State Department spokesman also issued this revealing statement referring to a warning issued to Israel in the run up to the intercept, "We emphasized caution and restraint given the anticipated presence of civilians, including American citizens," referring to the leftist anti-Israel cobelligerents aboard the boats.

If the terrorists that the Obama administration was attempting to help had used such restraint, Alisa Flatow would still be alive. In 1995, Flatow was a 20-year-old college student from

West Orange, New Jersey who was killed in a terrorist attack. Flatow was not in Israel to make a political statement or provoke anyone. Unlike those Americans on the flotilla, she was just there to visit. Tragically, like hundreds of victims of Hamas since, including other American citizens, she was murdered in cold blood by the very terrorists Obama is sending our money to now. Israel defends itself and gets the back of Obama's hand, but terrorists who have not only killed Americans and Israelis, but who have explicitly declared their intention to drive the Jews right into the Mediterranean Sea are rewarded with financial aid.

The United States has, since 2001, listed Hamas as a "Specifically Designated Global Terrorist" organization. In the world community, or what passes for it, this is supposed to mean that there is a high price to pay for providing support for such an organization, yet there was Obama committing the American people's money to provide "humanitarian supplies" to Hamas.

Even the *New York Times*, which tends to be sympathetic to terrorists, seemed confused about Obama's announcement: "The details of how the aid would be used in Gaza remained unclear. Nor was it immediately clear how Mr. Abbas, who has authority in the West Bank but not in Gaza, would be able to administer it."[23]

But, according to the *Times*, "White House officials said the money would be spent on housing, schools, efforts to provide access to drinking water and other health and infrastructure projects."[24] Even assuming some nonexistent way to ensure that was all the money would be spent on, using American dollars to provide for the basic services in Gaza that should be their own government's first priority, frees up Hamas's other money to buy weapons, and more sophisticated means by which to smuggle them into the Gaza Strip. No more raggedy flotillas for these terrorists.

Further obscuring American loyalty to her allies, Obama also used the Abbas visit to attack Israel's security blockade, declaring, "There should be some ways of focusing narrowly on arms shipments rather than focusing in a blanket way on stopping everything and then, in a piecemeal way, allowing things into Gaza." What an utterly stupid statement. Has anyone ever explained to Obama what smuggling is?

Obama's own statement acknowledges that supplies still reach Hamas-controlled Gaza, but that Israel just searches the incoming vessels to insure that the cargo isn't going to be used to kill people. Apparently, Obama thinks there is some other way to find weapons and explosives disguised and hidden among "humanitarian supplies," apart from looking for them. Here's a novel thought: How about you get no supplies at all until you stop smuggling weapons and murdering innocent civilians? That is the whole purpose of having labels like "Specifically Designated Global Terrorist Organization" and "State Sponsor of Terrorism."

The *New York Times* reported that international aid organizations "working in Gaza have warned of growing hardship. Deprived of raw materials, local industry has been severely damaged, and the Gaza economy has collapsed."[25] This account seems to suggest that the world has abandoned the poor, innocent Gazans, and conveniently leaves out their having gone to the polls and freely elected Hamas agents to run Gaza. So, these "poor victims" elected representatives for themselves whose stated objective is to annihilate the Jews. But, we should feel sorry for them anyway because their war against Israel is causing them hardships. After Republicans won back the House of

Representatives in 2010, restrictions were placed upon funds being sent to the Palestinian Authority and Gaza. Secretary of State Hillary Clinton and, at times, Obama himself, has violated the House restriction and sent the money anyway.

Obama and his liberal pals here always tell us the vilest crime in the world is racial discrimination. And yet, they take our money and give it to people whose sole objective in life is to exterminate a race of people. Welcome to Obama's world.

Aaron Klein reported before the 2008 election that Hamas leader Ahmed Yousef had endorsed Obama. Few Americans know that Yousef had been a covert Hamas operative inside the United States for years. In 2003 and 2004, I tracked him and his activities and found him using several aliases, operating mostly in Northern Virginia. In 2004, I confronted him and informed him that I knew who he was. He denied that he worked for Hamas, and then promptly fled the country. Two years later, he turned up in Damascus, Syria as a senior Hamas leader.

President Obama is either completely ignorant of the war Islamic terrorists such as Hamas are waging against us, or worse. Until we know more, I have the unfortunate task of reporting that we are now, officially, a state sponsor of terrorism.

After the first "freedom flotilla" failed, the praise and sympathy of the Obama administration inspired a second attempt – this one with even better political connections in the West, and a sassy new name for the project. One of the organizers of this was longtime Obama friend and ally Rashid Khalidi, and as an apparent demonstration of clout, they named this boat "The Audacity of Hope." Like many of Obama's close friends, Khalidi is notoriously anti-Israel to the degree that Obama's relationship with him could have threatened his 2008 election if the *Los Angeles Times* had released video tape it possessed, in which

Obama spoke at an event held in Khalidi's honor. The *LA Times* did report on the event, but refused to release the tape.

Writing in the *National Review Online* in the summer of 2010, former federal prosecutor Andrew McCarthy explained the relevance of this relationship and how comfortable Obama was in relationships with extremists: "Obama and Khalidi's mutual friends, the former Weather Underground terrorists turned professors Bill Ayers and Bernardine Dohrn, were also reportedly in attendance. (When Obama and Ayers teamed up to dole out money at the leftist Woods Fund, a $75,000 grant was given to the Arab American Action Network (AAAN) founded by Khalidi and his wife, Mona. Mona Khalidi has also signed the appeal for money to support The Audacity of Hope voyage. The AAAN regards Israel as illegitimate and has sought to justify Palestinian terrorism.)"[26]

At the time, McCarthy also pointed out that there could have been criminal charges filed against those responsible for the so-called Audacity of Hope flotilla, that is if the Obama Justice Department were interested in stopping terrorists' resupply efforts. "The United States has neutrality laws against things like fitting, furnishing or arming vessels with the intent of committing hostile acts against a country with which the U.S. is at peace. (Challenging a blockade is a hostile act.) We also have laws against providing material support to terrorist organizations like Hamas." During the 2008 campaign Obama used the phrase "we are the ones we have been waiting for."[27] It appears though that Obama and his friends were lying in the weeds waiting for us.

A Department of Justice that would prosecute such crimes as aiding and abetting a terrorist organization probably wouldn't help Hamas' parent organization, the Muslim Brotherhood, take over a nation such as Egypt. But that is precisely what associates of Assistant Attorney General Thomas Perez did. The Executive Director of Perez's former organization announced that he was teaming up with the Muslim Brotherhood in the run up to the overthrow of the Egyptian government. To the point, Thomas Perez was president of Casa de Maryland, a group known to advocate for illegal alien rights, just prior to joining the DOJ. The group's current Executive Director, Gustav Torres, is also on the board of directors of a left-wing extremist group called The Organizers Forum. This group chose to ignore the organic democracy movement made up of many pro-U.S. demonstrators, and declare the unpopular Muslim Brotherhood as the winner of the rulers' roulette game in Egypt.

"Our fall 2011 International Dialogue will be located in Egypt where we will meet with labor and community organizers and other activists in Cairo. There are exciting changes and developments that are currently taking place in Egypt with elections coming soon to determine leadership transitions in what has been an autocratic regime, now challenged by the Muslim Brotherhood," read The Organizers Forum website during the spring of 2011.[28]

But the Muslim Brotherhood came to the rebellion late and waited on the sideline for the chaos there to provide them an opportunity to use its signature method, violence, to take control of this strategically situated country. The Organizers Forum provided legitimacy to the Muslim Brotherhood at a time when it should have been delegitimized. What was so strange about The Organizers Forum is its declaration that the Muslim Brotherhood was the group opposing the "autocratic regime," when in fact, informed analysts indicated that it was not – at least not until their experienced, well-connected, community organizer brethren arrived from the United States.

The Organizers Forum board of directors reads like a who's who of Obama associates including: Mary Gonzales, Associate Director of the Gamaliel Foundation; and Wade Rathke, Chief Organizer of ACORN, just to name a few.

There has been a lot of confusion and misinformation reported about the Muslim Brotherhood in the media since the uprising and ultimate overthrow of the Mubarak regime in Egypt. To be clear, for years, counterterrorism experts both inside and outside of the U.S. government have sought to have the Muslim Brotherhood listed as a Specially Designated Terrorist Organization by the State Department. Most consider it the godfather of all violent terrorist organizations, having founded HAMAS and al Qaeda. Ayman al Zwahiri, who was al Qaeda's number two until Osama bin Laden's death, was a leader in the Egyptian Muslim Brotherhood, which had been outlawed in Egypt for violent extremism. Their record includes an assassination attempt on President Hosni Mubarak in 1995.

Bruce Tefft, a retired CIA officer and a founding member of the CIA's counter terrorism bureau told me, "The Muslim Brotherhood created the PLO and HAMAS," and counts among its membership "both al Zawahiri and [the deceased] bin Laden." The Egyptian Muslim Brotherhood is also the chapter that spawned Mohamed Atta, the ringleader of the September 11 attacks.

When Obama visited Cairo in 2009, many noticed a strange move by the administration to invite members of the Muslim Brotherhood to attend his speech. Typically, these are the kind of people that the Secret Service would screen out of presidential appearances. In June of 2009, *Fox News* reported, "Khaled Hamza, editor of the Muslim Brotherhood Web site, confirmed to *FOXNews.com* that 10 members of the Brotherhood's parliamentary bloc received official invitations to attend the speech."[29]

Obama's pattern of behavior since being elected president has made the bizarre seem normal. There has been a notable increase in cooperation between left-wing groups in the United States and violent Islamic terrorist organizations in the Middle East. Obama seems, inexplicably, to associate with both. Imagine dancing between two such disparate and dangerous organizations as Bill Ayer's Weather Underground and the terrorists of Hamas, two radically different factions joined only in their hatred of Western Freedom.

This strange pattern raises questions about what exactly the anti-American Left has in common with radical Islam. Hyperbole aside, the answer lies in their mutual hatred of the United States. And Obama seems to have far more in common with them than he does with any patriotic American.

Chapter 5

Reading Between the Lines

In addition to the other dubious endorsements from Muslim extremists in the Mideast, in 2008 Obama picked up the curious endorsement of Muammar Qaddafi. Before anyone was suspicious of the sources behind Obama's record-shattering $745 million campaign—really, before anyone was even aware of how prodigious Obama would become as a fundraiser—Qaddafi seemed to have an insider's knowledge. In a speech carried by al Jazeera on June 11, 2008, as translated by The Middle East Media Research Institute (MEMRI), Qaddafi revealed how pleased the Muslim world was with Obama: "All the people in the Arab and Islamic world and in Africa applauded this man. They welcomed him and prayed for him and for his success, and they may have even been involved in legitimate contribution campaigns to enable him to win the American presidency."[30]

Did Qaddafi know something that no one else even suspected at the time? Sometime after Qaddafi's speech, other evidence surfaced showing that Obama raised significant sums from sources in Qaddafi's neighborhood, including the tens of thousands of dollars the campaign claimed to have returned once it was revealed it originated in the Hamas-controlled Gaza strip. Following the 2008 election there was very little interest in the sources of Obama's massive fundraising, even though there was plenty of evidence of fraud.

Qaddafi's prescient speech didn't end with his apparent knowledge of Obama's sources of campaign funds. MEMRI's translation also included Qaddafi's foreknowledge that Obama's campaign rhetoric about supporting Israel was just a head fake also.

"But we were taken by surprise when our African Kenyan brother who is an American national, made statements [about Jerusalem] that shocked all his supporters in the Arab world, in Africa, and in the Islamic world... As you know, this is the farce of elections—a person lies and lies to people, just so that they will vote for him," Qaddafi stated in his speech that got no coverage from the main-stream American media.[31] Since his election, it has been pro-Israel Americans who have been shocked at how quickly Obama's policies turned hostile toward Israel, such as hundreds of millions in aid for Gaza after they attacked Israel with mortars in late 2008, forcing Israel to negotiate with Hamas and demanding that those negotiations begin with a return to the pre-1967 borders.

With the precision of a campaign insider, Qaddafi also predicted an Obama policy regarding Israel nearly a year before it happened: "We thought he would say: 'I have decided that if I win, I will monitor the Dimona nuclear plant, and the other WMDs in Israeli's possession."[32]

In May 2009, a State Department official announced that the Obama administration would pressure Israel to sign the Nuclear Non-proliferation Treaty that would allow Obama to inspect Israel's nuclear weapons program, something the Israelis have kept secret since its inception. A May 7, 2009 article in the Israeli newspaper *Haaretz* described Obama's demands this way: "If Israel fails to heed Washington's instructions on the diplomatic front, the press said, it will be punished in the most painful way possible - by having the so-called 'nuclear option' removed from its deck of cards."[33]

What is most amazing is that the propaganda arm of the Middle East, the anti-American al-Jazeera network, has proven more informative about Obama's Middle East policies than the sycophantic American media.

Just before the State Department announcement that the administration would be selling out Israel, President Obama bowed to King Abdullah of Saudi Arabia at the G-20 Summit in April 2009 and then, strangely, denied that he did. Despite the evidence (a video and multiple still photos) confirming the bow, the mainstream media asked us, "Are you going to believe Obama or your lying eyes?"

But Obama obviously bowed, with such great reverence that some described it as "Obama bowing to the keeper of his holy places." And this was weeks before Obama went to the Middle East and reclaimed his Muslim heritage. Just to be clear about the source of Obama's Muslim heritage, since the mainstream media goes on a full-throated attack against anyone who mentions Obama's name and "Muslim" in the same sentence, the source of this description came from the Obama administration. This is how *ABC News* reported it in a June 2, 2009 web article titled "The Emergence of President Obama's Muslim Roots": "During a conference call in preparation for President Obama's trip to Cairo, Egypt, where he will address the Muslim world, deputy National Security Adviser for Strategic Communications Denis McDonough said 'the President himself experienced Islam on three continents before he was able to—or before he's been able to visit, really, the heart of the Islamic world—you know, growing up in Indonesia, having a Muslim father—obviously Muslim Americans (are) a key part of Illinois and Chicago.'"[34]

His speech in Cairo was like a Muslim debutante's coming-out party. He said about himself all the things no one else was allowed to say about him before the election, when some Americans had reservations about electing a president so steeped in Islamic culture while the nation was at war with Islamic fundamentalists: "So I have known Islam on three continents before coming to the region where it was first revealed. That experience guides my conviction that partnership between America and Islam must be based on what Islam is, not what it isn't. And I consider it part of my responsibility as President of the United States to fight against negative stereotypes of Islam wherever they appear," Obama told the audience in Cairo. Some have excused statements such as this, saying Obama is simply trying to relate to all the peoples of the world so he can bring them together and declare an end to all wars.

Obama stated, "As a young man, I worked in Chicago communities where many found dignity and peace in their Muslim faith" Obama said. Unfortunately the terrorists who bombed a hotel in Pakistan less than a week after his Cairo speech ended apparently didn't get Obama's message that they are members of a peaceful and dignified religion. Perhaps he doesn't realize that many in his audience believe "world peace" means a global Islamist government subjugating everyone to a caliphate, which is a bit strange for someone who claims to have such a complete understanding of Islam.

The Cairo trip also had an awkward stop in Saudi Arabia, just weeks after Obama's infamous bow, perhaps so Obama could have the king greet him in broad daylight to show Americans back home that he didn't bow—a sort of do over, that he surely thought would Photoshop the original out of our memory. And he apparently didn't bow this time—or at least not literally. But just days before his trip, he genuflected to the Saudi royals and subordinated American victims of the Sept. 11, 2001 attacks as though they were subjects as well.

The Obama Justice Department argued that family members of the victims of the terror attacks should not be allowed to sue the Saudi royal family for helping finance al Qaeda. The lawsuit, filed in federal court by survivors of the victims, accused the Saudi royals of financially backing al Qaeda through direct contributions and donations to "charitable" front organizations set up to sponsor terrorism, according to documents insurance companies provided on behalf of victims and surviving family members of the attacks that killed 3,000 Americans.

The legal brief, filed on behalf of Obama by then Solicitor General Elena Kagan, stated that "the Supreme Court had historically looked to the executive branch to take the lead on such international matters because of 'the potentially significant foreign relations consequences of subjecting another sovereign state to suit'," according to the *New York Times*.[35] It is not surprising that Obama would appoint someone so confused about the role of the judicial branch to the Supreme Court.

In fact, to clarify the Executive branch's position on such matters, Democrat President Bill Clinton signed a law that allows victims of terrorism to sue foreign governments. The "Flatow Amendment" to the Foreign Sovereign Immunity Act (named for one such victim, Alisa Flatow) was intended to provide relief for the families affected by terrorism by allowing civil legal pursuit of state sponsors of terrorism. What the Saudis have done by supporting al Qaeda is a textbook example of the type of case this amendment was put in place to allow.

One might think that there would be a reasonable explanation for Obama taking this position, something that could at least provide him some political cover. There is not. Obama simply chose to side with the Saudi princes over their American victims. Kagan's argument that the State Department handles these matters better is ridiculous. It is a judicial matter, not a diplomatic one. Ironically, the Obama administration argued that terrorists captured on the battlefield deserve their day in a U.S. court, but they are now officially on record insisting that American victims of terrorists do not.

Besides, if Justice had remained silent on the issue, a court of law—not Obama—would have been the authority to decide whether the Saudis were liable. And if they are, as the suit contends, the American people have a right to know, and the victims and their families the right to be compensated. The Justice Department's argument did not overturn a court decision; it went so far as to ban the court from even hearing the evidence.

Democrats have been curiously silent regarding Obama's affection for the Saudis, especially considering the fact that when Bush was president, his relationship with the Saudis was a constant source of conspiracy mongering.

Sen. John Kerry sought to exploit Bush's need for Saudi cooperation in the war on terror in the 2004 election. In April of 2004, the Associated Press quoted Kerry using cryptic innuendo to infer that Bush had an unholy alliance after he met with Saudi officials: "I don't know if it was a deal, I don't know if it was a secret pledge, I don't know if it was just a friendly conversation among friends," Kerry said, "The fact remains that whatever it was, the American people are getting a bad deal today."

And who could forget the Democrats' favorite film of that year, Michael Moore's "Fahrenheit 9-11," which masqueraded as evidence of the Bush administration's complicity with the Saudis in the 2001 attacks. And they did all of this while somehow claiming that Bush was the one exploiting the war for political advantage.

Obama has declared whose side he is on; and of course, the Democrats have proved to be as duplicitous on Obama's relationship with the Saudis as they are on most everything else.

Obama does have a soft spot for some Americans; take late-term abortionist George Tiller, for example. Obama's remarks upon hearing that Tiller had been shot: "I am shocked and outraged." Contrast that with his statement on the news that 13 unarmed soldiers were gunned down at Ft. Hood Army Post by Nidal Hasan: "I would caution against jumping to conclusions" Obama said about the motives of the gunman. What it really comes down to is Obama being quick to publically damn any violent act that can be pinned on his own political enemies on the right side of the spectrum, while preaching patience to prevent Americans from rallying together against our nation's actual enemies.

Immediately following Hasan's deadly rampage on November 5, 2009, Obama's Homeland Security Secretary Janet Napolitano took to television airwaves to announce that her Department is now working to deflect any backlash against American Muslims following the terrorist attack committed by a Muslim soldier. This is the same Napolitano that issued a report earlier that year cautioning against the domestic threats of "right-wing extremism" and right-wing groups that might use issues such as abortion as a recruiting tool. Were Obama and Napolitano concerned about backlash against pro-life advocates in the wake of Tiller being shot? As it turns out, they should have. Although you would not have heard it from the mainstream media, pro-life activist James Pouillon was killed—with no news coverage whatsoever—just a short time after the massive coverage of Tiller's murder.

The media, except for *Fox News Channel* and very few others, played right along with Obama's Fort Hood narrative, failing to mention reports that Nidal Hasan screamed "Allahu Akhbar" as he murdered more than a dozen and wounded twenty-nine other unarmed soldiers. Imagine how Democrats and the media would have exploited the opportunity to smear all Christians as violent radicals if the man who shot Tiller had yelled "Hail Mary" as he opened fire.

U.S. Army Chief of Staff, General George Casey further promulgated this bizarre approach on the Sunday talk shows following the attack saying, "I am worried...that this increased speculation could cause a backlash against some of our Muslim soldiers."

So far, there have been two incidences of Muslims murdering their fellow soldiers in the peaceful confines of a military base or encampment. There is not one single solitary incident of a non-Muslim soldier shooting an American Muslim soldier to date. So why is it that when a Muslim shoots dozens of his fellow American soldiers Obama, Casey and the media are concerned for the safety of Muslim soldiers?

It would seem that the non-Muslim soldiers are in more danger than our Muslim soldiers. We're now allocating resources to try to protect Muslim soldiers that would be better spent shifting policy to try to keep radical Islamists out of our armed forces. And of course we will be told that we must recognize the importance of sensitivity to Muslims in the military, after all, many of them are translators for the languages spoken by the radical Islamist enemy. I don't suppose it ever occurred to General Casey that if Islamist soldiers would murder their fellow non-

Muslim soldiers that they might also sabotage the translation of documents and communications of the enemy.

The real problem with the Obama administration's handling of events such as this is that it is further evidence that they simply do not understand Fourth Generation Warfare: the type of non-military tactics the jihadists are using against us. If we recognize this act of internal treachery for what it clearly and obviously is, an Islamic jihad attack from within our own ranks, then we deny the enemy a propaganda victory. We can deter them from claiming Americans "are turning on their own" which allows them to recruit more Islamic extremists to carry out these attacks.

When the first Islamic attack occurred in the 101st Airborne Division by Sgt. Asan Akbhar, many warned of the enemy within. I was one of them. In an April 2003 article in *Insight Magazine*, I quoted former Assistant Secretary of Defense Frank Gaffney: "If [extreme] Islamists have infiltrated into the [armed] services it is a matter of grave concern because, by definition, Islamists are engaged in advancing an agenda that is inimical to this country and what it is and what it stands for, and its security most especially."

The Islamic jihadists who are waging this war against America want our soldiers to feel unsafe where they sleep. The tragedy is that our own military commanders, under orders from civilian leaders, may allow them to succeed. When the president justifies the Islamist cause with statements like "I would caution against jumping to conclusions," and announces that Muslims would receive special protection—implying that Americans are dangerous and the Muslims are victims—it encourages more attacks.

The most tragic part is how unlikely it is that there is a scintilla of sincerity in Obama, the Democrats, and their left-wing patrons' constant criticism of the way President Bush conducted the Global War on Terrorists. How could there be? Compare the behavior that the Democrats criticize in our national security forces' treatment of terrorists to their own behavior towards fellow Americans who weren't accused of anything.

The Democrats and their enablers in the media politicized the "enhanced interrogation" issue for their personal advantage. Since the Global War on Terrorists began, captured jihadists have claimed that they were tortured, and of course Obama, Democrats, and the media automatically took their word for it—even after we recovered a terrorist training manual that instructed captured terrorists to claim they were tortured. The Left's selective outrage over claims of inhumane treatment from brutal terrorist jihadists is itself revealing. These are the people who refused to believe Paula Jones, Juanita Broderick, Kathleen Willey and others when they said they were sexually harassed—and, in the case of Broderick, raped—by Bill Clinton. But when terrorists claim, just as their manual instructs, that they were "tortured" by their American captors, the same people demand an investigation and wail about the injustice of it all.

"Shamefully we now learn that Saddam's torture chambers reopened under new management, U.S. management," said now deceased Democrat Senator Edward (Teddy) Kennedy in 2004. This is an impressive rush to judgment for a man who was never adjudicated for allowing a young woman to drown after he drove off a bridge and saved himself. You might say that Kennedy "water boarded" Mary Jo Keopeckne to death. No one has accused any American interrogator of allowing a terrorist to die during enhanced interrogation, and Miss Keopeckne had not harmed anyone. And, in terms of inappropriate activities with younger female co-workers, he may have even trumped Clinton. And, by the way, couldn't the press corps' treatment of Linda

Tripp be considered far more degrading than anything the CIA is accused of doing to a terrorist?

Remember when Clinton's peccadilloes were on the front page in the late 1990s? There would be a dangerous aspirin factory in Africa that would have to be targeted with cruise missiles so Clinton could claim he was a "president at war" and therefore unassailable. We all know how the Democrats feel about undermining the president during wartime. Why, to do so is practically a war crime itself—well, that is, as long as the wartime president is a Democrat and thusly at war for the wrong reasons. Clinton had multiple opportunities to shoot missiles at Osama bin Laden, but refused. The attacks on September 11, 2001 could have been averted if only Clinton had been in political trouble during the times the bin Laden unit of the CIA had him in the crosshairs and simply needed permission to take him out. In 1999, on the eve of Clinton's impeachment, he began bombing U.S. ally Yugoslavia who was battling with Islamic terrorists, claiming that the Serbs were committing war crimes against the Islamic Kosovar Albanians. Speaking of torture, wouldn't ordering the bombing of hospitals and historic sites be considered war crimes? Few in this country are aware of this, but several NATO allies were complaining that that is what they were being ordered to do. Not that the mainstream media would have informed anyone of this, after all, the Serbs were traditional allies of the U.S. Apparently, in order to qualify for mainstream media protection, you must be a sworn enemy in desperate pursuit of killing American civilians.

Memo to the brave men and women whose job it is to defend America: Use Democrat Party tactics when pursuing an enemy—but first recognize that you must pretend that you are mocking America while you are defending it, otherwise you will be hauled in before the Democrat inquisition and tried for excessive jingoism, which is how the Left defines defending America.

Following Clinton's lead as Commander-in-Chief, Obama's political calculations take priority over what is good for our national security forces. Obama's signature accomplishment, killing Osama bin Laden, we now know had a built-in safety net for Obama in case something went wrong. Former Attorney General in the Bush administration Michael Mukasey, writing in the *Wall Street Journal* put it bluntly: "A recently disclosed memorandum from then-CIA Director Leon Panetta shows that the president's celebrated derring-do in authorizing the operation included a responsibility-escape clause: 'The timing, operational decision making and control are in Admiral McRaven's hands. The approval is provided on the risk profile presented to the President. Any additional risks are to be brought back to the President for his consideration. The direction is to go in and get bin Laden and if he is not there, to get out.' Which is to say, if the mission went wrong, the fault would be Adm. McRaven's, not the president's."[36]

Of course, after the operation was a success, Obama wasted no time in awarding himself the credit in a White House speech that famously contained dozens of "I"s, "me"s and "my"s, but not so many "McRaven"s.

Although the U.S. got bin Laden, we are losing Afghanistan. But you won't see Obama take any responsibility for it—nor will the liberal media hold him accountable. On May 13, 2012 *The Guardian* newspaper in the United Kingdom reported that there have been more than forty-five attacks on NATO soldiers in the past five years by people in Afghan military or police uniforms— the very people we are training to take over once NATO forces pull-out based on Obama's time table. A significant number of these attacks have occurred since December of 2009 when Obama announced a troop surge and also the date of evacuation.

The Guardian reported, "Jim Murphy, the shadow defence secretary, told Sky's Dermot Murnaghan that the recruitment process of Afghan recruits needs to be re-examined as Britain moves towards the withdrawal of nearly all forces in 2015. 'There has been a real emergence of these horrific attacks by people dressed in friendly uniform. This tells us that we should look at the recruitment processes again. My concern is that in 2015, when Britain is going to be running training regimes in Afghanistan, who is going to be ensuring the security of British personnel then?' [Murphy said]."[37]

This Afghani version of the successful Iraq surge was likely to fail from the beginning because Obama's military strategies always seem to revolve entirely around political calculations. Just before his announcement of his Afghanistan strategy in December 2009, *CBS News* reported, "Mr. Obama formally ends a 92-day review of the war in Afghanistan Tuesday night with a nationally broadcast address in which he will lay out his revamped strategy from the U.S. Military Academy at West Point, N.Y. He began rolling out his decision Sunday night."[38]

Roughly six months later Obama relieved his hand-picked General, Stanley McChrystal, not for failure of the mission, but for insulting Obama's personal pride. At the time, there were dual messages put forth by Democrats and their not-so-silent brethren in the mainstream media. Firstly, President Obama's swift dismissal of Gen. Stanley McChrystal demonstrates his solid command of the military, his decisive nature, and his commitment to success in Afghanistan. Secondly, that McChrystal is just one more cobwebbed item on a forgotten back shelf of the

Presidential pantry, another staple of the Bush administration, whose expiration date has come and gone.

Both narratives are absurd, dishonest to their core, and are co-dependent for credibility. Let us now dissolve them both, and place the blame—where it belongs, but will never be—on Obama.

The controversy started and ended quickly with a *Rolling Stone* article that hit the news circuit in June, 2010. Gen. McChrystal and his aides were quoted criticizing Obama. For example, one aide remarked of McChrystal's first meeting with Obama: "It was a ten minute photo op. Obama clearly didn't know anything about him, who he was. Here's the guy who's going to run his f----- war, but he didn't seem very engaged. The boss was pretty disappointed."[39]

Obama then issued his royal summons to Gen. McChrystal. He was careful to assert that he would need to speak with him "in person" prior to making any final decisions regarding his continued command of the Afghan war effort.

If any of the court stenographers who comprise the majority of the White House Press Pool were convinced by this supposedly detached, unemotional reserve, they should have been paying closer attention to imperial mouthpiece at the time, Robert Gibbs (and to give proper credit, ABC's Jake Tapper clearly was paying attention). For it was the sneering, dour Gibbs who delivered the public shiv in the ribs to McChrystal, saying it was as yet undetermined whether McChrystal was "capable and mature enough" to lead the war effort in Afghanistan. Ouch. Harsh words—and also a compelling testament that Gen. McChrystal's fate was sealed well in advance of his half-hour meeting with President Obama.

A White House disingenuous with the facts, willing to stage, manage and choreograph an important meeting, the outcome of which has already been decided? Loaded with precedent, hardly newsworthy, you say? Perhaps. But the real question should be: If Gen. McChrystal is incapable and immature, whose responsibility is that? And whose failure? Whose leadership, experience and judgment are called into question? Regardless of where they try to stop the buck, in this case there is absolutely no one to blame but Obama.

Contrary to some of the whispers at the time, issuing forth like so much gas from Democrat operatives and media mouthpieces, Gen. McChrystal was never "Bush's guy." He is, and has always been, Obama's man. Twelve months earlier, he was being hailed in the media as Obama's "hand-picked" replacement of Gen. McKiernan. Never mind that it had taken Obama more than half a year after that to reveal and articulate a plan for the war in Afghanistan—a plan that looked very much like the Bush plan.

Never mind, too, that Obama had met with his general less than a handful of times, most famously—and for only the second time in McChrystal's then four-month tenure—on the tarmac in Copenhagen, as the president engaged in an unsuccessful flyby of lobbying on behalf of Olympic host-city hopeful, Chicago.

Is this evidence that Obama is committed to the war effort in Afghanistan? Hardly. A sound reason for ignoring, then marginalizing and isolating your seasoned commander? Not a chance. A demonstration of Presidential command? Absolutely... in this administration.

Gen. McChrystal was Obama's handpicked general to run the war in Afghanistan. When Obama's handpicked General started thinking and speaking for himself, Obama fired him—and hired

President Bush's handpicked General, David Petraeus. The same Gen. Petraeus who devised the surge in Iraq—the same wildly successful surge in Iraq that was at first dismissed by Obama, and then grudgingly, barely, reluctantly acknowledged by Obama to be a "moderate" success.

And so, like much of the controversy that surrounds this administration, we're once again confronted with elements of pure tragedy wrapped in moronic comedy. Obama's tactical mistake was an elementary one; he stepped in his own trap. McChrystal complained to the media because Obama had failed to properly equip his Army, and so, on the eve of the most important tactical operation in years—the Kandahar Surge—Obama takes away his Army's leader, too. That should help them succeed without proper equipment. This is military leadership?

Did Obama relieve McChrystal in order to strengthen our position in Afghanistan? To buoy troop morale? To assuage the often fungible commitment of the Karzai regime? Nope. He did it solely in an attempt to save his face in the polls. The enduring salient point remains, Obama tapped a Bush veteran—a veteran he once assailed publicly—to lead the way in Afghanistan. The only certain outcome here is that Obama now, definitely, "owns" this command.

Chapter 6

Birds of a Feather Do Have a Political Agenda

"Part of my responsibility as President of the United States to fight against negative stereotypes of Islam wherever they appear." -- Barack Obama June 4, 2009 Cairo, Egypt

Who would have thought that Obama would expand the job description of the Commander-in-Chief to include public relations flack for the Muslim Brotherhood? The founders and promulgators of modern violent Islamic extremism have seen their legitimacy boosted significantly by Obama in many ways. One in particular is the proposed Ground Zero Mosque, the idea for which rose to prominence in the summer of 2010.

"As a citizen, and as president, I believe that Muslims have the same right to practice their religion as anyone else in this country. That includes the right to build a place of worship and a community center on private property in lower Manhattan in accordance with local laws and ordinances." Obama issued that endorsement in August of 2010 at an iftar dinner held at the White House with several Muslim Brotherhood-sponsored organizations represented. Many of them wrote glowing reviews such as this:

"President Obama spoke for the first time on the controversy surrounding the construction of 'Cordoba House,' a proposed mosque and Islamic Center in New York City, New York. Some are calling this one of the most courageous acts taken by a president lately. ...More than 100 Muslim leaders from around the world joined President Obama at Friday's White House iftar, including ISNA President Dr. Ingrid Mattson and ISNA Vice President Imam Mohamed Magid. Muslim diplomats from around the world, political, religious, and community leaders were also in attendance at the dinner. ISNA President Dr. Ingrid Mattson states, 'ISNA thanks the President for his strong and articulate support of the Muslim community and our rights here tonight.'"

This endorsement of Obama's "courage" came from a statement issued by the Islamic Society of North America. According to the Investigative Project on Terrorism (IPT), ISNA has a history and a record in the extremist Muslim community: "ISNA remains an unindicted co-conspirator in the Hamas-support prosecution of the Holy Land Foundation for Relief and Development." And, says IPT, ISNA is of the same pedigree as its sister organization the terrorist group Hamas. "ISNA was created by members of the Muslim Brotherhood—a radical Egyptian movement that seeks to spread Shariah law globally—in the U.S. many of those founders remain in leadership positions with ISNA. It invites controversial speakers to its nationwide conferences, including some of the world famous Islamists and advocates of Jihad," reports IPT, which maintains a comprehensive database of Islamic extremist groups.

The Western tradition of religious tolerance is under constant assault from Democrats, while they simultaneously defend the expansion of Islamic intolerance. And Obama has bestowed legitimacy upon the very extremist organizations that our federal law enforcement agencies are battling. The two front people for the Ground Zero mosque, Imam Feisal Adbul Rauf and his wife, Daisy Khan, reveal the political side of the Islamist movement. Soft-spoken and articulate, they are faithfully "on-message" with their stated aspirations to help "bridge" the cultural divide, and to be regarded as the "anti-terrorists."

Rauf and Kahn are nimble and seemingly non-threatening. The more pleasant and reasonable they seem, the more unfair their critics seem as they "rush to judge all Muslims as terrorists." The success of the political Islamic movement relies on their societal targets being confused by what they are seeing. In this case, Rauf and Kahn are also the lucky beneficiaries of a compliant and un-inquisitive media that not only refused to vet the motives of these two to see if their background matches their conciliatory story, but forgotten their own previous interviews that would have revealed a darker side.

Rauf and Kahn were never asked to reconcile Rauf's post-9/11 assertion that America was an "accessory" to the terrorist slaughter of 3,000 of her own, their refusal to disclose the sources of the $100 million they are raising, or their malleable condemnation of "terrorism?" And is their apparent condemnation of terrorism conditional, such as it is with many who identify with political Islam? Also, what about Rauf's refusal to denounce the violent terrorist group Hamas as a terrorist organization?

These would seem the salient questions; and yet, these queries were never made during the "interviews" to which these two submitted. If only their "mainstream" inquisitors would dig as deep within the Muslim community as they do looking for any trace or nuance that could be construed as "racism" among the "tea parties."

Rauf and Kahn's public retreat from the use of the term "Cordoba House"—with its unmistakable historical reference to an Islamic culture that celebrates military victories by eradicating all traces of its enemy (and most importantly, that vanquished enemy's religious culture) by erecting a mosque as an enduring monument to the Supreme Power of Islam—certainly bespeaks a sophistication about "communications framing" that you aren't likely to find in many "men (or women) of the cloth." So, let there be no doubt, these two are exceptional.

The more we uncovered about the Ground Zero mosque, the more it seemed to be a "Trojan Mosque"—and Rauf and Kahn the soft side of a larger objective to erect a monument at the site of what the Islamists see as a military victory. There is also evidence that Muslims have targeted the United States for an expansion of the Islamic movement's objectives overall. Those objectives involve building mosques and using them as a type of "settlement," the kind of settlements for which Muslims will justify terrorist acts when they are built by Jews in Israel. Seem far-fetched? Consider the drastic spike in mosque construction from 2000 to 2010. In a single decade the number of mosques in the United States spiked a staggering 74 percent—from 1,209 in to 2,106.

While the media only looks at the Ground Zero mosque's critics to find "the real motive" for opposition, it never looks beyond the superficial, happy, public relations face of the Muslims involved. Tayyip Erdogan, the Islamist Prime Minister of Turkey, is fond of reciting this poem which clarifies the role that planting mosques play in reaching the Islamist objective of Muslim dominance of the world: "The mosques are our barracks, the domes our helmets, the minarets our bayonets and the faithful our soldiers..."

These tactics are consistent with the history of Islamic political movements. It is also how the modern Islamist movement uses a tactic called Fourth Generation Warfare (4GW) to undermine nation states. A 4GW army is comprised of people who place a higher loyalty to an organization, tribe or religion than they pledge to a nation state and its laws, which is why it is no surprise that Islamists have publicly acknowledged adopting the tactics of 4GW to wage its war against the West. In an open society, we are never exactly sure who the enemy combatants are because they may not shoot at us, or blow something up. They might smile and say "all we want is peace" while provoking you and stretching the limits of your societal tolerance, leaving their targets confused. All the while, never defining what they mean by "peace."

Islamic extremists know our vulnerabilities and take prompt advantage. Their soft weapons are political, social, and psychological. To combat their advantage, we would have to sacrifice the freedom that forms the foundation of our society and culture. The Islamic extremists are equally confident we'll never take this route either. But look at the havoc their mosque proposition caused: Are we a nation that allows religious freedom to the point where we will accept this dualistic monstrosity overlooking the site of three thousand dead Americans who were killed in the name of the religion that now towers over their graves? Are we willing to subordinate our own First Amendment in order to send the message that we are not buying their "bridge to peace" nonsense as the reason for their act of provocation? On this very issue, the global leaders of political Islam had us right where they wanted us, especially after knowing that Obama and the Democrats would take their side.

Is this evidence that Obama is some kind of crypto-Muslim? No, but it does point out that Obama has found commonality with other anti-American extremists, and to that end they seem to have a common enemy. And his obsession with political correctness in military matters leaves America completely defenseless in the Muslim propaganda war.

Part II

The Corrupt Party, The Weak Party, and the Emergence of Crony Fascism

Chapter 7

Money for Nothing and a Scapegoat for Free

Liberal Democrats in Washington have put so-called "Wall Street Greed" on trial, but what do they have to offer in its place? Centralized power and control of the economy, which rests—what a coincidence—in their hands. For years, Democrats have been running successful election campaigns against the "straw men" they have created on Wall Street. The Democrats rail against big corporations who have escaped regulation, but aren't they the people who wrote the regulations? Is it any surprise that those corporations that do manage to escape regulations are usually found to have been big Democrat donors? To define terms, when I refer to Wall Street greed, I am not referring to people, through corporations, who pursue success within the free market economy. To be clear, I am referring to the people and corporations that use their financial resources to sponsor corrupt politicians to protect them from legislation that will adversely affect their competition. In this environment, Democrat lawmakers and the "greedy" Wall Street types they pretend to be at war with are codependent. Those who slop the hogs, so to speak, in Washington know that their survival depends upon keeping the government hogs well fed. And in fairness, that type of Wall Street greed, even in its worst incarnation, is far better than its ugly, venal cousin—government greed.

In the spring of 2010, during the debate over Obama's so-called "financial reform" bill that ultimately became known as the Dodd-Frank Bill, Democrats benefitted mightily by gassing the myth that Republicans are "the party of Wall Street," flush with corrupt banker cash, desperate to stymie justice, and eager to craft a reform bill that conforms to Wall Street's specific wish list. That is the rhetoric that Democrats used to intimidate weak Republicans into allowing this bill to pass congress, although, in fairness to the Republicans, their only way of stopping it was a filibuster.

"Bipartisanship for Republican leaders means bringing Wall Street to the table, bring Wall Street banks into the room, and let them help you write the legislation." That is what left-wing Senator Sherrod Brown, a Democrat from Ohio told *Politico* during Senate debate.

This is akin to Eliot Spitzer blackmailing a prostitute, Nancy Pelosi calling someone else a lunatic, or Bill Clinton ascribing "political" motives to an electoral opponent. But the Democrat narrative on Wall Street—the corrupting influence of cash, and which party wallows most in the trough—is just as ludicrous, and just as blatantly dishonest. And, make no mistake; it is the only narrative on the subject. The Republicans are too timid, too disorganized, or just too outright pathetic to fight back and force the Democrats to defend Wall Street's special channel to the Democratic Party. One Democrat strategist described it to me this way, "Wall Street buys the Democrats and gets the Republicans for free." Translation: Democrats are political prostitutes and Republicans, being prisoners of free market ideology, are afraid to sound the alarm over Democrats' duplicity, even though what the Democrats are doing at the behest of their corporate donors is a violation of free market principles.

While the debate was raging over the financial reform bill, I advised several Republican Senators that they should demand a special prosecutor be appointed to investigate the already documented connection between President Obama, Wall Street financiers and the Congressional Democrats who had been loudly posturing about going after "big business, bankers, and Wall Street." The objective was to expose corrupt Democrats and their benefactors and change the dishonest narrative that the Left has used for years. But that advice was ignored.

A *Real Clear Politics* article from April of 2010 showed that in 2008, Goldman Sachs employees were Obama's second largest donor group, while Citigroup and JPMorgan Chase also made the top ten. Logically, this doesn't square. Democrats have been publicly assaulting the free enterprise system for years, and yet have simultaneously remained the biggest recipients of Wall Street cash. *Real Clear Politics* also reported in 2010 that "Goldman employees have donated more to Democrats than Republicans in every election since 1989."[40]

After the 2008 elections, Democrats finally had the votes, the political coverage and the compliant press required for them to fashion legislation that would provide them greater control over the financial sector. Democrats could now choose which businesses succeed and which ones do not, tightening the noose around the financial sector, and strengthening the hangman in Washington with one hand on the rope and the other extended for a payoff. The favored corporations are rewarded with special legislative exemptions that make it more difficult for their competitors. This doubly favors the largest banks, which can afford both the required payoffs and the new legal requirements that make the cost of doing business too high for smaller businesses. So in the end, the very "big business" that Democrats claim to hate is the direct beneficiary of big government. "Goldman chief Lloyd Blankfein, like Citigroup's Vikram Pandit, has expressed support for financial reform," says *Real Clear*

Politics.[41] Is this a Festivus miracle? Have the Democrats written such fantastic financial regulations that even the biggest banks gave it the stamp of approval? No. Unfortunately, it's a modern-day spoils system, designed by shameless, corrupt, and duplicitous legislators, and signed into law by a protégé of Saul Alinsky.

So, while the financial reform bill was being written, some of Wall Street's giants were lining up to pay for protection from it. And it wasn't long after passage of the bill intended to prevent risky Wall Street investments that a big Wall Street bank, whose CEO is a friend of Obama and of course a major donor to the Democrats, lost a huge sum—in risky investments. In May of 2012 it was revealed that JPMorgan recklessly lost two billion dollars. Reuters reported that the financial reform bill the Democrats passed to prevent such things had a special caveat: "The 2010 Dodd-Frank financial oversight law enacted in response to the financial crisis includes the Volcker rule, which bans banks from making speculative bets with company money. But it includes an exemption for trades done to hedge risk."[42]

Special exemptions are now so common, the Left's favorite attack phrase, "crony capitalism," can no longer be honestly used as a pejorative. It used to be the Left's favorite description of free enterprise system, when it was a lot freer than it is today. They don't use it so much anymore given their increasing stake in its ownership. That term is no longer operative. The more appropriate term, "crony fascism" is, unfortunately, far more accurate in describing the political class' relationship with certain big businesses.

It's so Machiavellian and so strategically brilliant that under other circumstances one couldn't fail to be impressed by it; Democrats have been blackmailing Republicans for the very corruption the Democrats themselves own. And the Republicans are too terrified of Obama and the liberal media to seize the issue and clobber the Democrats over the head with it.

Most Republicans in power refuse to acknowledge it: Democrats assume this populist issue of Wall Street "reform," for show only... and to continue extorting large piles of cash from big business. It's like a pro-wrestling match, where the fight is fake, but the payoff is real. Too real.

And yet, the solution is simple. Republicans, who were well outnumbered in both the House and Senate at that time, could have simply demanded a special prosecutor to investigate Obama's relationship with Goldman Sachs and Wall Street, the taxpayer bailouts and the individuals who profited from them, and the corruption at Fannie Mae and Freddie Mac—for which Rep. Barney Frank, for one, has never been held accountable, and for which the Democrats were directly responsible. When the Democrats objected, as they inevitably would have, the Republicans could have accurately called it a cover-up and demanded that the Democrats come clean.

Not only would this have allowed Republicans to take back the high ground from the Democrats—and set the stage for a productive, national lecture to the Democrats regarding the corrupt big business/big government nexus—it would have been the rare political move with the benefit of actually being good for the country. Imagine, a win for Republicans and a win for America! This would also have set the stage for the 2012 presidential election which will be argued in the same framework— government managed economics versus the free enterprise system.

The night before Senate Majority Leader Harry Reid forced Republicans to capitulate on the Dodd-Frank ill, he took a break from attacking the GOP as the party of big business, so he could jet up to New York and extort the Wall Street firms he'd spent the week softening up with threats of government action. Then, with his reelection campaign coffers newly topped off, he returned to Washington. And, as the *Politico* reported, "Reid took his criticisms a step further … calling Republicans 'anti-American' for blocking the Wall Street reform bill."[43] And in response, how did the Republicans defend themselves? They sheepishly agreed to allow debate on the bill—thus foregoing their only method of stopping it—as though they were the ones with something to hide.

In short, Republicans sold out the free market for fear of being labeled "fascist" by the real fascists, because the Dodd-Frank Bill is another layer in the foundation for this new era of "Crony Fascism." It gives Democrats--along with their lefty allies on Wall Street—the power to finish destroying the free enterprise system that they have spent the last two decades battering with ceaseless meddling through Fannie Mae, Freddie Mac and other government programs that award control of the free market to politicians in Washington.

And to those who think "Republicans are in on it, too"—why would the Democrats let the Republicans muscle in on their racket? As it stands now, Democrats get all the loot and Republicans get all the blame. Republicans are rarely effective in getting their side of the story out. Democrats, with lots of help from their liberal friends in the mainstream media, have always been able to drive the debate over government corruption scandals and park it on the Republican side of the aisle, regardless of where it belongs.

When a bipartisan scandal comes to light, Republicans get 90 percent of the blame, and every Democratic scandal somehow ends in hand wringing over the dishonesty on both sides of the spectrum. Take, for example, the People's Republic of China and Democratic National Committee fundraising scandal of the 1990s. President Clinton and the Democrats were caught taking millions of dollars in campaign donations from communist China at the same time the Clinton administration was helping China access key defense technology that has helped them fast-forward several generations on their weapons of mass destruction systems that now threaten China's neighbors and the United States.

The Democrats and the media repeated the irrelevant argument that the problem was in the way political campaigns were financed. We were told over and over that the problem with the campaign finance law is not what is illegal. It is what is legal.

That argument led to the campaign finance reform laws known as McCain-Feingold. What the Democrats did in the 1990s had nothing to do with the need for reform: taking laundered donations from foreign countries was illegal then, just as it is illegal under the new campaign finance standards. But by changing the debate from what Clinton did to what Democrats claim is wrong with the way campaigns are financed, the public's attention was redirected—and so too their outrage—from what could have been a criminal investigation of the Clinton administration for bribery (or worse) to one of bipartisan campaign finance reform. It is this template that we saw employed once again in the 2008 election of Obama with regard to the bailout of the banking industry brought on by the failures of Fannie Mae and Freddie Mac.

Journalists and Democrats are engaged in a full attack on the concept of a free-market economy that started with the economic crash of 2008, and four years later is the lynchpin of Obama's reelection strategy. Of course, they say it's the capitalists who are to blame for attempting to make a profit in the home mortgage industry. That is how Democrats are framing this scandal and anchoring it to the Republicans who, for the most part, have failed to launch any type of counter-attack. If Republicans point to Fannie Mae and Freddie Mac as examples of the very type of government control of the economy that Obama claims to be the solution to the country's financial woes, Obama would be forced to defend the consequences of his brand of government. Those failures are a clear example of the federal government having one hand in the legislation and regulation of the lending industry and the other hand in the cookie jar. That kind of debate would convince even socialists that government power corrupts politicians.

In the six years prior to the financial crisis, the Bush administration, as well as Sen. John McCain and others, warned of a potential financial crisis if Fannie Mae and Freddie Mac weren't reined in from their very liberal lending policies. But those warnings were met with visceral attacks from leading Democrats, such as Barney Frank, who suggested that managing Fannie and Freddie responsibly amounted to an attack on poor people.

It's no wonder they defended government involvement in the private mortgage business so vociferously: Fannie and Freddie were heavily subsidizing the re-election campaigns of Rep. Frank and Senators Christopher Dodd, Barack Obama and others. But even worse, after the scandal broke it was revealed that former Clinton administration officials such as Franklin Raines and Jamie Gorelick were paid tens of millions of dollars for holding executive positions at Fannie and Freddie. Members of the very political party that constantly deride citizens pursuing profits in the private sector as "fat cats"—profits that in many cases, aren't even close to what these "government cats" were making.

So, in addition to providing a campaign war chest for House and Senate Democrats, Fannie Mae and Freddie Mac were used as a personal piggy bank for former Clinton administration officials needing a soft landing. This is business as usual in fascist totalitarian governments around the world. Cronies of the government's leadership get rich off the nation's treasury while its citizens jockey for preferential treatment in the "redistribution" of what is left. And in those corrupt nations, just as it was in the case of Fannie and Freddie, it's all done in the name of helping the poor.

McCain's failure to push back against Obama during the 2008 campaign is where he lost the election. In the first debate between the two, Obama's opening statement included this vicious and erroneous attack: "Now, we also have to recognize that this is a final verdict on eight years of failed economic policies promoted by George Bush, supported by Senator McCain, a theory that basically says that we can shred regulations and consumer protections and give more and more to the most, and somehow prosperity will trickle down. It hasn't worked. And I think that the fundamentals of the economy have to be measured by whether or not the middle class is getting a fair shake. That's why I'm running for president, and that's what I hope we're going to be talking about."

If McCain had responded with a direct confrontation of Obama such as, "Senator, the American people know that I have forcefully criticized President Bush when I felt it was necessary, but this is not Bush's fault. The public record is replete with their warnings and mine, for Congress to take action. Neither is it a failure of the free market economics. This was a failure brought on by a government-backed institution that was abused by members of your party for personal gain to the tune of hundreds of millions of dollars. And Senator, instead of heeding the president's and my warning, you chose not to stand up for what was right. Instead you chose to take hundreds of thousands of dollars from Fannie Mae and Freddie Mac for your own campaign and looked the other way on corruption."

If McCain had gone on offense over the economy, and the actual root causes of the financial meltdown, the 2008 election would likely have turned out differently. But therein lies the problem with the weak party, we are never sure if they really understand the principles they are supposed to represent.

Chapter 8

Lost Opportunities to Regain the Public's Trust

The Republicans saw dramatic victories in the 2010 midterm elections. It was utter revulsion with Obama and the Democrats' rein of superiority that drove the American people to the polls to mitigate the unbridled power the Democrats were claiming for themselves after the 2008 elections. Republicans gained 63 seats in the U.S. House of Representatives and six seats in the Senate. Just two years earlier, the Republican Party had practically been written off as no longer relevant. Unfortunately for the Republican establishment, the election results did not constitute an endorsement of any kind, but rather the only other option for voters growing weary of the Democrats. Reluctant Americans went to the polls and voted for Republicans as the default choice of a desperate nation—the last hope of stopping the devastating attacks on our freedoms and economy from the Democrat power structure led by Obama, Pelosi and Reid. Sadly, many Republicans already serving saw that wave of anxiety as their ticket to the reins of power and lacked sensitivity to what that election meant. It simply didn't matter to them that the new Republican bosses would be the same as the old Republican bosses—the ones that failed to recognize America's right and proper demand for a return to Constitutional Government.

Republicans had an opportunity to do something extraordinary, something exemplary, novel, even—an act of sincerity that would have established a bond between the GOP and their voters, as well as potential converts. Something to demonstrate that they "got it," that their commitment to the Americans who put them in office was real. Republicans, upon assuming power, should have nominated an incoming freshman to be Speaker of the House. It would have been a bold move, but also the kind of move that could remake the GOP in the image of the country. It would have loudly announced that the new Republicans recognized that the people of this nation want to govern themselves and not be slaves to political establishments—from either party. It would be a clear-cut announcement that the people run the country.

I proposed this idea in September 2010, but knew the idea would not be well received by the leadership-in-waiting because they, like the Democrats, believe they are entitled to power—that it is their turn. They won the election lottery and put in their time, so they get to sit in the big chair and dictate the seating arrangement. So, it was just "one of those things," a chance for elected officials to be bigger than politics—an opportunity for Republicans to demonstrate good faith in the American people by truly choosing one of them to lead The People's House; a window to show that they are serious about reforming Washington, and, perhaps most importantly from a political perspective, they could have changed the status quo and kicked the image the Democrats and their brethren in the news media have crafted of the GOP as the "Good ole boy" party of Washington insiders— no better than the image Americans have started to discern of the Democrats. There were many well-qualified potential leaders among the field of newly-elected Republicans across the country. Some have led young men into battle and created a track record of subordinating their own interests, including preservation of life and limb, to the greater cause of the principles of their nation. Of course, this idea was met with the usual cynicism of "you don't understand, running the House of Representatives is so hard it requires decades of experience." But, we Americans see what all that experience has done for the country. This is a concept few, if any, Washington Republicans understood, even though it would not only have been good for the country, it would have been a brilliant political strategy.

Democrats had a head start in framing their targets and sharpening their attacks against who they knew would become the Republican leadership. But if the new leadership had not been part of the old Republican establishment, the Democrats' attack strategy would have been left toothless. A freshman speaker would have forced them to attack an American, one of the people they have been ruling—not part of the political ruling class. This would have truly exposed the Democrats for exactly what they are—anti-American elitists—and the American people would have rallied around an American under attack by the establishment. It would have further exposed the Democrats' war on America's freedom and their desire to be our rulers instead of our government.

That momentous action would have sent a clear message to the American people that the establishment elite had been disenfranchised and that regular Americans are the special interest of the new GOP. But instead, they ignored the people and immediately walked from their decisive election victory right into a Democrat trap.

The Democrats made a big show of Obama's first State of the Union address following the 2010 election. Fresh from being stripped of power in the House, and stripped of legitimacy to govern by a wave of anti-establishment sentiment, the Democrats needed to make Republicans smell and look like them. They wanted Republicans to be seen by the American people as being in the same club, the establishment club, of which Democrats are the permanent potentates. They wanted to rob voters of their sense of satisfaction for having changed the complexion of the political class by showing that their votes had changed nothing. Democrats wanted to send a message to those voters: "If you think this election made any difference, look at your Republicans... they are already groveling to us." So, Democrats publically asked Republicans to sit with them at the State of the Union address rather than be divided by party, as is the tradition. This would show Americans that they didn't really gain anything, Republicans are just like them. And Republicans clumsily fell right into the trap, most likely out of fear that if they didn't, they would look too much like those "dangerous" Tea Party members. But, establishment Republicans were anxious to get the stain of common-American off, and join the ruling aristocracy once again. Democrats knew that the majority of Americans saw them as the "establishment," and now, in one of their very few acts of conciliation, Democrats pretended to extend an olive branch. Unfortunately, it was draped in poison ivy.

It is important though to distinguish between the Republican establishment in control of Congress—those that obtained rank through seniority—and real patriots who are frequently frustrated by the compromisers who stifle good ideas out of fear of angering Democrats and the media. One such patriot is Louie Gohmert, Congressman from Texas. At the end of 2008, and after the first disbursements of the Troubled Assets Relief Program (TARP) there was a sum of about $350 billion in unspent TARP funds. Gohmert came up with the idea to use the TARP money to "electrify the American economy" by declaring a "tax holiday" for U.S. taxpayers in legislation that would use the remaining unspent bailout funds to provide a tax-free period for those who had paid for the bailouts.

Gohmert, at the time in his second term, said of his proposal, "We can save more home mortgages, increase employment, and boost economic growth for a lower price tag with this plan than with any centralized bureaucratic program, all by giving the power back to the taxpayers."

Clearly, it was an idea borne of frustration. "I am sick of Washington millionaires trying to decide which of their cronies should get the next wad of taxpayer money," Gohmert said.

Gohmert's frustration, and his plan, took business-friendly tax cuts and melded them to the anti-bailout sentiment among taxpayers who had been paying their own bills and were suddenly forced to pay the freight of those who did not. A free-market populism of sorts. Although it says a lot about where we are economically as a nation when we view allowing taxpayers to keep some of their own money as "populism".

Gohmert's proposal struck a chord with those who recognized that bailouts are the opiate of financial institutions that pocket the reward of risky investments and dump the losses on the taxpayers through bailouts. Gohmert's bill picked up 56 cosponsors, but ultimately proved too aggressive for the timid GOP. If Republicans had been smart, they would have grabbed hold of Gohmert's idea, sharpened it to a point, and dared Democrats to stand in front of it.

What a powerful image that would have been: The Democratic Party, that rode to power on a platform of class warfare, caught turning their backs on the people they claim to represent—the middle class—in order to help the very billionaires they have taught their constituents to hate.

Political posturing aside, Gohmert's idea should have been embraced by Republicans because it was the right thing to do for the taxpayers. And, as he also pointed out, the plan made more economic sense than bailing out large corporations: "Those in lower-income brackets who are hit the hardest by the FICA tax would see huge money back, and could then choose who should benefit from their hard earned money. Even the self-employed and small business owners would receive a fantastic amount of their own much-needed money, and they will be able to invest that back into their businesses and even create the ability to hire more people."

Repeatedly, Republicans have missed such opportunities to strike a chord, not only with their base of constituents, but with all working people who would have seen an immediate benefit from the payroll tax holiday. Republicans should have been embracing ideas that promoted freedom and that would connect with more working people, including independent voters. Then, once the Republicans had their attention, they could have made the case for the advantages of a limited federal government. Additionally, this plan could have helped Republicans reclaim the mantle of free market economics that they forfeited by backing the bailout to begin with. It would have left the Democrat hypocrites looking more like Boss Tweed than their idol Robert La Follette.

Chapter 9

Job Openings for Scapegoat Herders

On Aug. 15, 2011 President Obama announced a campaign gimmick that he thought would make him look like Harry S. Truman running against a "do-nothing Congress." But his version came with an extra-partisan twist—it was designed to help Obama to avoid responsibility for his high unemployment numbers which, at the time, seemed poised to continue all the way through his first term and end up hanging around his neck like a millstone going into the 2012 election.

"I'll be putting forward ... a very specific plan to boost the economy, to create jobs and to control our deficit. And my attitude is get it done. ... And if they don't get it done, then we'll be running against a Congress that isn't doing anything for the American people and the choice will be very stark and very clear," Mr. Obama said to the unappreciative Midwestern rogues during his flyover-country bus tour just prior to jetting off to "the Vineyard," where a man of his effete charm would be better appreciated.

This was an unsophisticated trap for Republicans. If they refused to allow him his latest stimulus bill, then he was going to blame Republicans for his bad economy. Hoping that no one would remember his earlier "jobs bill," the 2009 American Recovery and Reinvestment Act, where he borrowed $787 billion to keep the unemployment rate from going over eight percent. Of course, unemployment went over nine percent and still has yet to drop below eight percent—which is why Mr. Obama needed a scapegoat. He might as well have said, "If they don't vote for my jobs bill, then I am not responsible for the unemployment rate. They are." If his "jobs" bill had passed the House of Representatives, it would have—just like his other stimulus bills—provided financing for his re-election by putting money into the pockets of his financial supporters, banana republic style.

There was nothing particularly clever about Obama's strategy, but it is one the Democratic militia in the mainstream media can work with. Savvy political observers will see right through this scheme, but Obama knew he could count on the media to portray it to 100 million voters in his voice. That is, it would sound more like Republicans attempting to sabotage Mr. Obama by not letting him "rescue" average Americans and put them back to work. The media would sell Obama's plan as a cure for unemployment if only those wicked Republicans, who really just want to see the president fail, would have gone along with it.

Obama's plan seemed also designed to get him out of another promise he made to fix the economy just after taking office: "If I don't have this done in three years, then there is going to be a one-term proposition," Mr. Obama said in an interview with NBC in February 2009. That guarantee was about to reach its expiration date. So, the plan was to find a way to blame Republicans for his failure, and generally, the way Republicans can never seem to defend themselves, it was likely to succeed. But the GOP could have put Obama back on defense, and helped him keep his 2009 promise if House Republicans had responded to Obama's 2011 politically stunted stimulus bill with this offer: "Mr. Obama, with the unemployment rate currently at 9.1 percent, we will pass your jobs bill if you agree to withdraw your reelection bid for president if the unemployment rate hasn't dropped below 7.8 percent one year from now." That would have put Obama's expiration date at about the time of the 2012

Democrat National Convention, when he would expect to be re-nominated.

This Republican counter-strategy would have not only highlighted the fact that unemployment under Obama had gone up despite his profligate spending, but would have forced him into the same trap that he attempted to set for Tea Party Republicans who tried to put the brakes on his mad spending spree.

Obviously, Obama would never have accepted such an agreement, but a counteroffer like this from House Republicans would have exposed him as a hypocrite and his claims as bogus. Democrats never expect the Republicans to fight back aggressively, which is why they expect to get away with tricks like this one. The Democrats are also always confident that the liberal media will always slavishly serve their interests. If Obama had a plan that would, as he put it, "create jobs" and help the American people, why wouldn't he stake his reelection on its effectiveness? This is the kind of sting that could have exposed Obama early in his campaign by pointing out that he doesn't believe in the efficacy of his own plans and that all he has to offer the people suffering in his economy are political tricks to help shift blame onto others. It also shows that no matter how great his plan is, or how many people he says it will help, it was not worth risking his reelection in order to get it passed. In other words, keeping his job as president is more important to him than actually helping the middle class. Once Mr. Obama's cloak of compassion was unraveled, independent voters would have seen him the way the rest of us always have: as a power-seeking narcissist enabled by the subservient liberal media.

Republicans usually cede the upper hand to Democrats, and that has been especially true in their dealings with Obama. It is as if they actually believe the left-wing media reports that

Obama is a noble and universally popular figure, and thus unassailable. That is why Obama's campaign team had no reservations about leaking to the *New York Times* that their campaign strategy is to go negative. Obama's strategists told the *Times* that they intended to say that, regardless of who it was, the Republican nominee's party caused the economic problems we now face. Obama tipped his hand publically in September of 2011 by again saying that the bad economy was going to be the Republicans' fault. This political equivalent of a Freudian slip revealed that Obama knew his economic plans were failing.

A *New York Times* report in June 2012 chronicled the economic blame redistribution while covering Obama on the campaign trail. "That day, Mr. Obama continued his weekly travels around the country, prodding Congressional Republicans to pass his 'to-do list' of temporary tax cuts and spending initiatives to help create jobs. The Republicans only mock him, which leaves Mr. Obama free to blame his opponents and their presidential standard-bearer, Mitt Romney."[44]

That raises an important question: If the economy had been doing well, would the President be giving Republicans the credit? Fortunately, that does not have to be a rhetorical question. Just five months earlier, in January 2012, there was a temporary uptick in the economy and a drop in the unemployment rate. Obama was out taking full credit in his State of the Union address: "The state of our union is getting stronger. And we've come too far to turn back now." He even boldly claimed that he was willing to work with the very Republicans that he had previously, and would again, blame for the bad economy: "As long as I'm president, I will work with anyone in this chamber to build on this momentum."

The Obama campaign also released a television ad at the

same time that heaped glowing praise on the President for his masterful handling of the economy. In part, the ad made these economically-suspect claims: "After taking office, President Obama signed the Recovery Act to help get our economy back on track. As a result: The U.S. has seen twenty-two consecutive months of private-sector job growth. The private sector added more than 3.1 million jobs over those twenty-two months and manufacturing added 334,000 jobs in the last two years, the first time since 1997 that manufacturing employment rose."

Interestingly, just five months before that State of the Union address, Obama was on record saying that if his 2011 jobs (spending) bill wasn't passed by Congress, the Republican-controlled House of Representatives would have to take all responsibility for the economy, or at least the part of the bad economy that he wasn't still blaming on former President Bush. It turns out that Obama has been somewhat shortsighted. To recap the dizzying changes in Obama's position on who is responsible for the economy: In September of 2011 he announces that if his new stimulus bill does not pass (it didn't) Republicans are responsible for the economy; five months later, the economy is picking up steam and Obama runs out to take credit for it; six months after that, the economy looks anemic again and Obama is back to blaming the Republicans. In short, Obama has indeed indicated that if the economy is good he gets the credit, if it's bad it is the Republicans' fault. It makes one wonder who is working on his campaign—former Pravda writers, perhaps?

Perhaps Romney should point out Obama's spastic duplicity and ask that he take a position on the economy, one way or the other. In fact, if Republicans had any moxie they would ask Obama this question: "If the Republican-controlled House was able to stop you from fixing the economy, why didn't the

Democrat-controlled House stop President Bush from wrecking it, as you claim he did?" Such questions could undo Obama's campaign strategy because it is a poorly rigged contraption that is almost entirely dependent upon the so-called mainstream media continuing to play along with Obama's contrived and alternating narratives.

Obama's strategy is also dependent on Romney being weak like McCain, and deciding to seek androgyny instead of clarity when it comes to explaining the difference between what the political Left says and what conservatives believe.

We frequently hear and read that presidential elections are won with votes from the middle that flow to the most moderate candidate. There was a moderate running for president in 2008 and a left-wing extremist beat him, so Republicans should stop taking advice from those who seek their defeat. What they are really running from is what the Democrats and their cohorts in the media will say about them. As John McCain learned, no matter how much they love you when you are up against other Republicans, they will hate you like they hate the rest of us when you are up against one of their own.

This is not the time for Republicans to "run to the center" where the political establishment claims the votes are. This is a time for bold statements that clarify our national purpose while appealing to the logic of voters by exposing the fraud of the Democrats' strategy to have the people who take from the system decide how the people who pay for the system's money is spent.

Republicans can start by explaining to the American people, especially those who have been previously inattentive, that what they hear about conservatives from the media and Democrats is a lie. There is polling evidence that many people are now ready to listen to an alternative view.

Democrat and independent voters are told by the Left that success is a euphemism for "greed." They hope that no one will notice that all of their schemes to redistribute the wealth of this country always end up transferring more power to the political class.

A close inspection will reveal that politicians use the word "greed" as a weapon to gain power while robbing people of their rights to liberty and property. "The President's reforms will guarantee that Americans never again end up holding the bag for the bad decisions and greed-driven policies of big banks and credit card companies—protecting consumers and taxpayers alike. Wall Street reform will protect taxpayers and investors by making the financial system more stable for everyone," reads Obama's website statement about the Dodd-Frank financial reform bill. That bill will choke the flow of capital by adding millions of dollars in costs for financial institutions just to file newly added paperwork for transactions. An analysis in *The Economist Magazine*, February 2012, regarding the Dodd-Frank bill stated, "There is an ever-more-apparent risk that the harm done by the massive cost and complexity of its regulations, and the effects of its internal inconsistencies, will outweigh what good may yet come from it."

So, government regulators are going to tell professional investors where the money they oversee will be safe. The same regulators who missed the $50 billion dollar ponzi scheme run by Bernie Madoff, and more recently the huge losses at JPMorgan and John Corzine's mf Global. In the end, Dodd-Frank gives the federal government and elected politicians more power—and power is the manifest greed of the political princelings of the Washington establishment. At the core of the financial meltdown, which was the catalyst for the Dodd-Frank "reform" bill, were two quasi government entities, Fannie Mae and Freddie Mac. Dodd-Frank does not touch them. They were already under government management when their lending policies triggered the financial crisis.

The lesson of recent elections is that we cannot keep electing moderate Republicans. We can't send moderates to negotiate with the left-wing extremists in the Democrat party—the net effect is the destruction of the Republic. The idea that Dodd-Frank would, as Obama says, ensure that "Americans never again end up holding the bag" for risky investments is ridiculous. Americans shouldn't have been responsible for bailing out the investment banks in the first place, that was big government's intrusion into private markets, and Obama participated in the decision to bail out the banks—even those that were not in trouble. The federal government has now, thanks to Dodd-Frank, assumed more risk than ever for financial failures of Wall Street. But now, the decisions regarding who gets bailed out have a much stronger political component. So now, Republicans are trying to "weaken" some of the more costly aspects of Dodd-Frank. Well, that provides us some prickly comfort. All we have gotten for electing moderates, like we are told we should, are solutions too small to fix the problems the Left creates. Many Republicans' only objection to Obama's healthcare bill was that "it went too far"—not that it was a terrible idea for the government to insinuate itself further into the free market for healthcare, which is what the government had been doing for decades and precisely why there were problems with the market. For every pound of progressive destruction, we get eight ounces of cure, at most, from our side. So, bit-by-bit, we lose our freedom to an ever-expanding federal monstrosity, which centralizes power within the political class, members of which use that power to make themselves wealthy.

The number one commodity in Washington is influence. The influence brokers force speech codes upon us so we are not allowed to use words like "socialism" to describe the socialists in the Democrat party because "that drives away independent voters." While they call us names like "Nazi" and "fascist," Republicans call them "our good friends and colleagues" in strict obeisance to the rules they have made for us. Then, the Left wins elections with a highly unpopular ideology (poll after poll shows that 40 percent of Americans identify themselves as conservative, while 20 percent identify themselves as liberal); and yet, our Republican establishment tells us we must compromise.

This idea of sending moderates to negotiate with the far Left has done enormous damage not only to the nation's economy, but to the very idea of free market economics. Compromise on everything from Fannie Mae and Freddie Mac to tax increases and regulation of the markets has led to disaster. But instead of Leftists taking responsibility for their failed redistributionist policies, capitalism gets blamed instead, even though the Left has been negotiating us out of our freedom for the past 100 years.

When we nominate the candidate the establishment wants us to, we lose every time. The Left gets most of what they want, and conservatives and capitalism get all the blame for the failures of those compromises. Obama's campaign strategy is to blame the bad economy on Republicans, but Obama can be defeated if Republicans have the temerity to put his leftist ideology on trial in the 2012 election, and explain how liberalism—not capitalism—brought the economy to its knees.

But first, Republicans have to recognize that it was their

own weakness, in the interest of compromise, that allowed too much liberal poison to choke a once strong and free economy.

Chapter 10

Is This the Change You Voted For?

Did spending three quarters of a trillion dollars fix the economy? Did it prevent the unemployment rate from rising above eight percent? That is what Obama promised in his first major initiative after taking office. The $787 billion American Recovery and Reinvestment Act, otherwise known as the "Stimulus Bill", was voted on and passed in February of 2009. No one had read the stimulus bill before it passed Congress, including the one who said it was absolutely necessary. "I feel such a sense of urgency about the recovery plan before Congress," Obama wrote in the *Washington Post* on February 5, 2009.[45] Perhaps he thought the mere magic of saying that he was going to spend that much money would fix the economy. I am not being facetious. Before no one had read Obama's healthcare bill, they neglected to read the stimulus bill when the House and Senate voted on and passed it, yet we were told over and over that if Obama wasn't given nearly a trillion dollars to spend immediately, the country as we know it would be finished.

"Our nation will sink deeper into a crisis that, at some point, we may not be able to reverse," Obama wrote.[46] It sounded more like an extortion racket, especially since Obama actually does have the power to tank the economy. The stimulus bill of 2009 should have laid to rest, once and for all, the Keynesian theory that government confiscating wealth and redistributing it stimulates the economy. Obama borrowed nearly a trillion dollars to pass out and to "fix" the economy and no one asked the question "what qualifies Obama to fix the economy, and if merely spending money fixes it, then the economy shouldn't be broken should it?" Spending was already at record levels. What experience does Obama have at fixing anything? He has never run a state, city, company or even a hotdog stand. The sidewalk vendors on the mall outside the White House have more business experience than Obama. Not that anyone would know that since the liberal media utterly ignored this lack of experience during the campaign, while simultaneously ridiculing Sarah Palin's lack of experience. The media refused to bring it up even after the election, when he was holding the economy hostage to get his $787 billion.

When asked whether increasing the deficit by nearly a trillion dollars would actually help the economy or not, Obama responded with a political attack on Bush referring to the deficit he inherited from the previous administration, without explaining why adding a trillion dollars to it was going to help anything. Shameful, considering Obama faithfully voted to increase that deficit while he was in the Senate. So much for the politics of "change." That retort revealed Obama's utter cluelessness about the economy altogether. If government spending is good, as in his stimulus bill, how could he complain about Bush's deficit? That was government spending, too. It is twisted logic—how the money is spent is irrelevant—whether it is spent on bombs to protect our citizens or solar panels that our citizens don't want.

What the debate over the stimulus bill really showed us is how Obama would use the economy he talked down before his stimulus package passed. If the situation improves he will take credit for fixing it and cite government intervention as the solution; if it worsens, he has already laid the groundwork to blame Bush, capitalism and free market economics. Despite his press releases, you can tell how Obama judges the effectiveness of his stimulus bill by his reelection strategy of continuing to blame Bush and the House Republicans elected in 2010.

Revealing their true intentions at the time, Obama's White House Chief of Staff, Rahm Emanuel, freely explained to the *Wall Street Journal* how the administration intends to exploit the recession. "You never want a serious crisis to go to waste. And this crisis provides the opportunity for us to do things that you could not do before."[47] That statement sounded like an amateur's conflation of Machiavelli and Hegel—semantically creating the crisis for drastic action that leads to the consolidation of power in their hands. And thanks to the House and Senate Democrats plus three so-called Republicans (one is now out of the Senate, the second will be out this year and the third will be out in 2014) they were awarded all the legitimacy a trillion dollars will buy.

After declaring an emergency with all the drama that the nation would be over if his stimulus bill didn't pass, one might think that Obama would be standing by to sign the bill into law, but he wasn't. The largest spending bill in history, despite all the hyped urgency, was subordinated to Obama's more important matters—namely, himself. He and Michelle jetted off to a three day weekend in Chicago to be seen in all the trendy spots. Did saving the nation from economic disaster interfere with his social schedule? Well, probably that too, but really to Obama this is all just political theater; the words mean nothing—it's all part of the show. That is how he is able to tell us one day how America would be over soon if he didn't get nearly a trillion dollars to hand out, and then go out on an excursion the next day, using our Air Force and Marine Corps equipment as his personal amusement park rides.

The stimulus was basically a platform for Obama to come out of the closet and shed his campaign image of a moderate Democrat. Obama's argument for the stimulus was based upon his belief that capitalism and free markets were a failed experiment. Obama wrote, "I reject these theories, and so did the American people when they went to the polls in November and voted resoundingly for change."[48] The American people did not reject freedom and embrace socialism by electing Obama because Obama did not run as a socialist. But even if he had, Obama's platform wouldn't represent change; it would represent all that is wrong with the economy—an alarming expansion of government power and centralized control of the economy.

The ways in which the stimulus funds were distributed were quite curious. Most Americans would have likely been outraged to learn that a Marxist group that has demanded the "destruction" of the U.S. and issued a call "to bring this government down" is the recipient of stimulus funds from Obama's American Recovery and Reinvestment Act of 2009 (ARRA). This same group, the Brecht Forum, has also called for the complete takeover of insurance companies and farms in America.

The controversial stimulus bill provided funds for the New York State Council on the Arts (NYSCA), which promptly granted the New York City-based Brecht Forum $5,000 in 2009 and $9,000 in 2010. The NYSCA had previously announced in 2008 that due to state budget cuts it would no longer be able to fund 573 organizations that it had previously funded. One of the groups on the list to be slashed was the Brecht Forum. After NYSCA secured $399,000 in stimulus money, the Brecht Forum once again had funding. The NYSCA, coincidentally, is chaired by Obama supporter Danny Simmons.

The Brecht Forum is host to the New York Marxist School and displays this statement on their website: "Can society be changed significantly for the better? What kind of changes would be needed? And, who could bring about such changes? Questions like these are what motivated Karl Marx and Fredrick Engels to develop a method for studying the dynamics of change in societies. In 1975, a group of civil rights, community, labor, and student activists came together to found The Brecht Forum's New York Marxist School. They saw the study of Marxism, as central, not as a dogma but as a living current of thought and as a vital tool for understanding capitalist society."[49]

In a September 2009 lecture at the Brecht Forum, Jed Brandt, a longtime communist, political activist and outspoken atheist offered the following instructions: "We have to bring this Government down! We have to help destroy this system and that requires increasing the alienation that working people and oppressed people feel. The way this change is going to happen is the destruction of The United States of America!"

Fox News Channel picked up on Brandt's call to action and played clips several times the week of March 1, 2010. My own investigation uncovered the link to federal stimulus dollars providing financial support for the Brecht Forum. The grants from NYSCA were ostensibly provided for artistic projects; for example, the NYSCA website shows the following as the description for the Brecht Forum grant: "The Brecht Forum's 09-10 program features workshops in the participatory theater techniques developed by the noted Brazilian director Augusto Boal. The program includes monthly workshops led by members of the Theater of the Oppressed Laboratory and two master workshops led by Augusto Boal."

The website for the Theater of the Oppressed Laboratory describes this form of art in rather revealing political terms: "Augusto Boal has defined Theater of the Oppressed as a rehearsal for revolution." The website further describes its mission as using "interactive theater as an organizing tool" and works with "educators, human service and healthcare workers, union organizers and community activists" to solve perceived problems.

In 2011 you could add to that list Occupy Wall Street protest organizers. Jed Brandt was one of the editors of the official OWS publications, "The Occupied Wall Street Journal." This link means that Americans tax dollars subsidized OWS, and that despite the media claims that it was an "organic" uprising of the people, it was really inspired by a Marxist front group, and had the endorsement of President Obama himself. "We are on their side," Obama said during an October 18, 2011 interview with *ABC News*.[50] That interview occurred after publications of the "Occupied Wall Street Journal" appeared bearing Brandt's name.

Just as the supposedly "organic" Occupy Wall Street protest was taking over a park near Wall Street, Obama began to step up his class warfare rhetoric, not only revealing his more socialist tendencies, but also his logical immaturity. In a speech on September 19, 2011, two days after the Occupy Wall Street kick-off, Obama announced the "Buffett Rule" and his willingness to use corrupt rhetoric.

"We have to prioritize... Either we ask the wealthiest Americans to pay their fair share in taxes or we're going to have to ask seniors to pay more for Medicare. We can't afford to do both. Either we gut education and medical research or we've got to reform the tax code so that the most profitable have to give up tax loopholes other companies don't get, we can't afford to do both. It's not class warfare, it's math," Obama said. But it is not math. It is philosophy—one of Aristotle's thirteen fallacies commonly known as the straw man argument. Obama makes up whatever he wants the conservative position on an issue to be, and then pretends to refute that non-existent argument by projecting himself as the defender of the downtrodden.

He came off as a pernicious Don Quixote tilting at productive people. Obama often uses unsophisticated fallacies to promote his illogical policies. "Either we raise taxes" on what he calls the "wealthy" or we will be forced to "gut education and medical research.... And schools that are crumblin [sic]," Obama said in a speech, during which he for some reason feigned a non-specific ethnic accent by dropping his G's. Obama's economic illiteracy is simplistic, but Republicans should have re-appropriated his absurdity and turned it around. In other words, they should have used his own class warfare arguments against him.

Here are a few examples of how conservatives and Republicans should have responded to his nonsense:

- Either we stop Obama from giving our tax money to fat-cat labor union bosses or our seniors won't get medical treatment.

- Either we stop Obama from pouring millions of dollars into the outlaw group ACORN and its subsidiaries or homeless families will be forced to sleep on the street.

- Children are going to bed hungry while Obama hands over stimulus grants to Marxist organizations such as The Brecht Forum who openly declare their plans for the overthrow of the United States.

- While our roads and schools and bridges are crumbling Obama is sending hundreds of millions of our tax dollars to the terrorist group Hamas.

- Either we ask Obama to demand that his millionaire and billionaire friends, like those at Solyndra who he gave billions of our tax money to, give it back, or Americans who play by the rules will have to do without.

- If people in America are ever going to get a fair shake, the Obamas must stop their conspicuous consumption of tens of millions to support their insatiable cravings for beluga, squab and other luxuries.

The Obamas use public funds to live like czars, flying their extended families to five-star vacations around the world and flaunting opulence as though it was their own money they burn, while so many Americans sleep in their cars because Obama hasn't created a single job.

This is just how Democrats play politics, by making it personal. The difference between these juxtapositions and the ones Obama offered are that these are accurate and fair comparisons versus Obama's which were contrived for the purpose of pitting one American against another. Even with the facts on our side, conservatives still have not learned to use the illegitimate tactics of the left to legitimately level the playing field.

Clearly, as President, Obama has relied on his roots as a community organizer, which is to say "social justice activism" and using social pressure to promote redistributionist schemes. During the campaign of 2008, Obama was disciplined with his message that he was a mainstream Democrat, and despite the abundance of evidence that he had maintained many relationships with extremists such as his pastor Jeremiah Wright and former Weather Underground terrorist Bill Ayers, the mainstream media refused to investigate and report to voters about those relationships. But analyzing what Obama has said as president reveals many things that Americans would find objectionable if explained in context. In fact, a December 2011 poll shows just how out of step Obama is with the average American. The Gallup poll reported that 64 percent of respondents considered big government the biggest threat to the nation, with only 26 percent that viewed big business as a bigger threat. In addition, 8 percent considered big labor the top threat to the nation. So it could be said, since Obama has been a stalwart ally of big labor, that 72 percent of the nation opposes Obama's governing philosophy.

Obama's own words leave a huge opening for Republicans to expand a debate that is long overdue, and place President Obama' economic philosophy under scrutiny and expose its illogical conclusions. In a CBS 60 Minutes interview in December 2011, Obama once again revealed that his view of the government is at odds with the desires of the governed. He said: "And it requires everybody to have a fair chance, everybody to do their fair share, and rules of the road that create fair play for everybody. And what people have been frustrated about, especially since the financial crisis, is the sense that the rules are rigged against middle-class families and those aspiring to get in the middle class. So, if we're willing to make investments in education so that everybody gets a fair chance and kids aren't coming out with $100,000 worth of debt to go to [sic] college."

The question is: who is it that doesn't have a "fair chance"? If you are poor in this country you get free meals and a free education from pre-school all the way through a bachelor's degree and, in many cases, free graduate school. We are constantly told about the high number of hungry children in this country, yet the high school dropout rate is the highest in the poor schools where students get a free breakfast and a free lunch.

How hungry can these children really be if they won't even show up to school to get their free meals? And Obama claims that the taxpayers who are picking up the tab for all of this have an unfair advantage?

If you are a standard top ten percent wage earner, your taxes are paying for someone else to get a better education than perhaps you are able to provide for your own children. That is called "social justice" in Obama's world. If Americans believe the "rules are rigged against the middle-class," they are right. But it is Obama now, and those predecessors who share his ideology, that have been writing those rules for decades. If you are in the middle-class, for example, you could not afford the size of donation that the wealthy partners at Solyndra gave Obama in 2008 that greased the skids for their government guaranteed "loan" that Obama favored them with after he got elected. Apparently that is Obama's idea of "fair play." Give a fairly large donation and you get to play with taxpayers' money.

That is just one example of how the Left's system of government-run economics has created the very disparity that Obama claims to care about. In its most cynical form, it is a protection racket that the political class in general, but mostly Democrats, has created that requires big business to pony up donations to the politicians that will be making the laws that can cost them immense sums of money.

So, yes, the deck is stacked in favor of big business, but it is Obama and his Democrat forbearers, that made it that way. With threats of punitive laws, the Democrats are able to extort political support from the big businesses that they claim to be against, as was the case with the Dodd-Frank bill. That is why Democrats get more Wall Street money than Republicans do. All the bluster about needing more regulation of Wall Street is just an announcement from Democrats that big business needs to line up and pay their alms to escape the regulatory burden contained in the next round of legislation. And if you are not big enough or don't contribute to the right politician, then you pay the price that government regulation costs you (but not your competitors who played the corrupt political game correctly).

In his speech at Osawatomie, Kansas in December of 2011, Obama leveled the following charge against an unspecified "they": "In fact, they want to go back to the same policies that stacked the deck against middle-class Americans for way too many years. And their philosophy is simple: We are better off when everybody is left to fend for themselves and play by their own rules."

This is Obama's perverted view of our constitutional right to self government—"everybody is left to fend for themselves." There is enough evidence in this one distortion to prove Obama's deviancy. With one line, "their philosophy is simple: We are better off when everybody is left to fend for themselves" Obama blots out the entire concept of individual liberty. But the line "play by their own rules" is astounding for its hubris. It is Obama and his fellow travelers who have always maintained that the Constitution is a document left open for them to interpret any way they please. In other words, Obama believes the law of the land can mean whatever he wants it to mean at any given time, yet he accuses others of wanting to play by their own rules. Obama also made this interesting observation in his Osawatomie speech, but failed to understand its significance: "You know, a few years after World War II, a child who was born into poverty had a slightly better than 50-50 chance of becoming middle class as an adult. By 1980, that chance had fallen to around 40 percent. And if the trend of rising inequality over the last few decades continues, it's estimated that a child born today will only have a one-in-three chance of making it to the middle class."

Of course, Obama blames this on people getting wealthier instead of the most obvious explanation—the exponential growth of government. During the time period Obama cited, government growth has far outpaced the expansion of wealth in the US, paradoxically with substantial sectors of government growth devoted to ending poverty. Ordinary logic prefaces the conclusion that bureaucratic strangulation of small business opportunities is by far the most likely reason fewer people are in the middle-class, as opposed to Obama's claim that some people's ability to succeed caused others to be left behind. Obama's unpopular philosophy requires his use of deception to make rhetorical points that are substantively false. In his self-serving and brutal assault on logic, his words and actions have forced us to suspect the worst about his motives.

Obama talks a good game about looking out for the average guy, but contrary to his sympathetic treatment of the Marxist tainted Occupy Wall Street protesters, when a real organic movement took to the streets, made up of working Americans, Obama mocked them. "Those of you who are watching certain news channels on which I'm not very popular, and you see folks waving tea bags around, let me just remind them that I am happy to have a serious conversation about how we are going to cut our health care costs down over the long term, how we are going to stabilize Social Security... But let's not play games and pretend that the reason [for the deficit] is the Recovery Act," a smirking Obama said, dismissing complaints about his stimulus bill in late April 2009, according to Politico.[51]

The irony of the Tea Party is that Obama is primarily responsible for the movement. His decision to borrow nearly a trillion dollars for his stimulus bill, his threats to force his healthcare bill on the nation, and his promise to "spread the wealth around" naturally made people nervous. Especially when they knew nothing about him, thanks to the media. People were already anxious after the 2008 economic crash; there was a palpable sense of unease. But few people saw it like Democrat pollster Patrick Caddell. "The people have had it with the political class," Caddell was saying to anyone who would listen—that was December 2008, before anyone else had noticed. What Caddell saw was a public growing weary of the massive debt and the bank bailouts. But it was Obama's arrogant condescension towards American values that seemed to enflame the passions and send people to the streets to have their voices heard. For most of the demonstrators it was the first public protest of their lives.

The movement is predominantly composed of a small number of Libertarians and a large number of Conservatives. The Tea Party Conservatives are formerly Conservative Republicans who have given up the notion of having a moral government and are tired of funding an immoral government. They are disconnecting from the Republican establishment, which today seems more comfortable managing big government than effectively reducing it. Herein lies their commonality with Libertarians. The Tea Party is thus at the vertex of this confluence that emphasizes as its central theme the notion that the U.S. must return to a Constitutionally-limited federal government.

The catalyst of this political migration is Obama's stated goal of a "fundamental transformation of America." Indeed, the Tea Party can most accurately be described as a popular revolt and instinctive response to such statements from this administration. Obama's speech on the national debt reinforced the logic behind the movement: the President's extremist economic goals further imperil our nation's already dire fiscal situation. Obama stated, "The fourth step in our approach is to reduce spending in the tax code. In December, I agreed to extend the tax cuts for the wealthiest Americans because it was the only way I could prevent a tax hike on middle-class Americans. But we cannot afford $1 trillion worth of tax cuts for every millionaire and billionaire in our society. And I refuse to renew them again. Beyond that, the tax code is also loaded up with spending on things like itemized deductions. And while I agree with the goals of many of these deductions, like homeownership or charitable giving, we cannot ignore the fact that they provide millionaires an average tax break of $75,000 while doing nothing for the typical middle-class family that doesn't itemize."

By referring to deductable expenses as "spending in the tax code," the President indicated his belief that a person's income is for the discretionary use of government, or for whatever Obama deems our nations "investments." This then clarifies the enormous difference between the beliefs of the contemporary Democratic Left and those of free-market capitalists. The former believe that an individual's labor product is a resource that belongs to the state, which may then be allocated, or, more accurately, appropriated in a manner that it sees fit; the latter argue that a person's labor belongs to them and them alone, and are thus the ultimate deciders of its fate.

This understanding puts Obama's philosophy of government control of resources and labor at odds with the framers of the U.S. Constitution, as Thomas Jefferson made clear in his first inaugural address: "A wise and frugal government, which shall restrain men from injuring one another, which shall leave them otherwise free to regulate their own pursuits of industry and improvement, and shall not take from the mouth of labor the bread it has earned. This is the sum of good government, and this is necessary to close the circle of our felicity."

Jefferson's words almost seem as though he anticipated Obama, whose argument for power is feeble compared to an argument for liberty. At every self reference in Obama's statements is a redirect of personal freedom transferred to his control. "But let me be absolutely clear: I will preserve these health care programs as a promise we make to each other in this society. I will not allow Medicare to become a voucher program that leaves seniors at the mercy of the insurance industry, with a shrinking benefit to pay for rising costs. I will not tell families with children who have disabilities that they have to fend for themselves. We will reform these programs, but we will not abandon the fundamental commitment this country has kept for generations."

The "fundamental commitment" that Obama speaks of is another straw man argument because it is not a promise that American citizens made to one another. Rather, it is a promise Obama and the Left made to people who take from the system, and a promise paid for by people who provide that system with money. This is possible because the voters who take far outnumber the voters who pay. Obama's promise is that he will use force to take from a few to provide for the many in exchange for their political support. This he calls "courage." It is also disingenuous, for it is not the widows and the orphans Obama really cares about, it is new power he can get for himself through exploitation of their conditions.

Today, fewer than 10 percent of Americans provide almost all federal income tax revenues. As it so happens, Obama and the Democratic Party's chief constituency is part of the 90 percent who think the top 10 percent can afford higher taxes. This explains why the Left defines democracy as the power for those who take from the system to decide how to spend the money of those who pay for the system. Over the years, this concept has been dressed up in all too many guises: social justice, economic justice, economic democracy, social democracy, and now "getting a fair shot."

The Tea Party emerged out of the fact that this narrow definition of democracy has grown steadily and unchallenged ever since Obama began campaigning for President. The Democratic Party has over decades built its base on a dependency class, while the Republican Party has provided only a modicum of resistance. This has set the national interest on a drastically divergent path and shattered American history's political status quo.

Most importantly, however, it has allowed for the rise of political migrants who desire a return to the founding principles that made our nation prosperous in the first place, and produced the wealth and power that the political class now seeks to redistribute to itself.

Chapter 11

Bringing Government Efficiency to the Auto Industry -- Obama-Style

Not content with nearly wrecking the economy while running Fannie Mae and Freddie Mac, Democrats decided to try their luck in the automobile industry. Democrats were anxious to get their hands into the grease because there were a lot of bondholders involved with wealth to redistribute to the overpaid union workers. Just as they did with Fannie and Freddie before the market crash, for the first year and a half, since Obama expropriated it, Democrats have been crowing about the wild success of the auto industry.

"And because they did, the American auto industry—an industry that's been the proud symbol of America's manufacturing might for a century; an industry that helped to build our middle class – is once again on the rise," Obama said in November of 2010.

"This is a case of the government doing what we should do. This is an American success story," said U.S. Senator Sherrod Brown, a Democrat from Ohio. But in June 2011, Cato Institute Economist Daniel J. Ikenson testified to the House Subcommittee on Regulatory Affairs and described a much different picture: "[C]alling the bailouts 'successful' is to whitewash the diversion of funds from the Troubled Assets Relief Program by two administrations for purposes unauthorized by Congress; the looting and redistribution of claims against GM's and Chrysler's assets from shareholders and debt-holders to pensioners; the use of questionable tactics to bully stakeholders into accepting terms to facilitate politically desirable outcomes; the unprecedented encroachment by the executive branch into the finest details of the bankruptcy process to orchestrate what bankruptcy law experts describe as "Sham" sales of Old Chrysler to New Chrysler and Old GM to New GM; the costs of denying Ford and the other more deserving automakers the spoils of competition; the costs of insulating irresponsible actors, such as the United Autoworkers, from the outcomes of an apolitical bankruptcy proceeding; the diminution of U.S. moral authority to counsel foreign governments against similar market interventions; and the lingering uncertainty about the direction of policy under the current administration that pervades the business environment to this very day."[52]

Basically, Ikenson labeled everything the Democrats have said about the auto-bailouts a lie. The rosy scenario painted by Obama and the Democrats would amount to fraud if the CEO of a publically traded company had said such things. But, unlike the criminal exposure public corporate executives face when they fib about earnings, there are no such consequences when the Democrats do the same thing.

"[O]nly the most gullible observers would accept GM's profits as an appropriate measure of the wisdom of the auto bailout. Those profits speak only to the fact that politicians committed over $50 billion to the task of rescuing a single company. With debts expunged, cash infused, inefficiencies severed, ownership reconstituted, sales rebates underwritten, and political obstacles steamrolled – all in the midst of a cyclical U.S. recovery and structural global expansion in auto demand—only the most incompetent operation could fail to make big profits. To that point, it's worth noting that more than half of GM's reported profit—$1.8 billion of $3.2 billion—is attributable to the one-time sales of shares in Ally Financial and Delphi, which says nothing about whether GM can make and sell automobiles profitably going forward," Ikenson told the Subcommittee.[53]

Ikenson also points out that there are deeper philosophical problems with the overall concept of U.S. government bailout and ownership of private corporations, such as the fact that the more successful auto producers are forced to subsidize their competition through their payment of taxes. And, perhaps most importantly, America has lost a measure of moral authority in the eyes of the rest of the world. Ikenson points out that the idea of expropriating corporations has international implications.[54] In other words, how can the U.S. government lecture corrupt third world governments about confiscation of private companies in places like the People's Republic of China? What if it is an American company whose assets are confiscated in one such country; will Obama explain to a skeptical foreign leader that only his own reasons were valid?

Allowing Washington to control auto giants can only ensure their ultimate failure and diminish the chances of those companies ever becoming productive and economically viable again. Obama's involvement did not even address the underlying cause of the failures – the United Auto Workers Union. A 2008 Heritage Foundation study concluded: "UAW workers earn $75 an hour in wages and benefits – almost triple the earnings of the average private sector worker. Detroit autoworkers have substantially more health, retirement and paid time off benefits than most Americans."

Obama not only refused to address the problem of excessive wages for auto workers, he used private equity and U.S. taxpayers' money to make sure that his union supporters felt no pain at all. Obama's use of tax subsidies meant that most Americans were forced to subsidize the salary and benefits of people considerably better off than themselves. When Obama and the Democrats talked about redistributing wealth, could anyone have possibly imagined they meant taking money from low-income taxpayers and giving it to people who make several times what they make?

Many economists recommended that Chapter 11 bankruptcy would have been the best thing to facilitate the needed reorganization of the troubled automakers. For one thing, it would allow them to renegotiate labor contracts that are more consistent with their competitors in auto manufacturing. But, instead of court supervised bankruptcy, GM and Chrysler got Obama-supervised reorganization, which meant that creditors that loaned money were forced, by Obama, to take huge losses—and even while they were negotiating how bad their losses would be, Obama went on the attack. In May 2009, *ABC News* reported that Chrysler's bondholders were feeling the heat from the White House: "Thomas Lauria, Global Practice Head of the Financial Restructuring and Insolvency Group at White & Case, told *ABC News* that [Obama Auto Czar Steven] Rattner suggested to an official of the boutique investment bank Perella Weinberg Partners that officials of the Obama White House would embarrass the firm for opposing the Obama administration plan, which President Obama announced Thursday, and which requires creditors to accept roughly 29 cents on the dollar for an estimated $6.8 billion owed by Chrysler."

ABC News reported that Bill Burton, the White House Deputy Press Secretary, denied it, saying "There's obviously no evidence to suggest that this happened in any way."[55] But contrast that denial with what Obama himself said about Perella Weinberg

Partners: "While many stakeholders made sacrifices and worked constructively, I have to tell you some did not. In particular, a group of investment firms and hedge funds decided to hold out for the prospect of an unjustified taxpayer-funded bailout. They were hoping that everybody else would make sacrifices, and they would have to make none," according to the *ABC News* account which also quoted Obama saying, "I don't stand with those who held out when everybody else is making sacrifices."[56]

ABC News also reported that Lauria is a heavy financial supporter of the Democratic Party, but quoted him as saying that Obama's threat that he doesn't stand with them, "Kind of sounds like 'You're fair game.' In whatever sense. People are scared. They have gotten death threats. Some have been told people are going to come to their houses. G-d forbid if some nut did something, I'm just wondering how the president would feel." Apparently, Obama wasn't worried about such backlash against people who disagree with him.

In light of the severe treatment that American investors received from the newly elected administration, it is necessary to ask in whose interest President Obama was serving when on March 30, 2009 he publically ordered Chrysler to either conclude a merger with Italian automaker Fiat within 30 days or lose federal bailout funds. That untimely announcement placed Chrysler in the untenable position of accepting whatever Fiat offered, cutting the legs out from under the struggling American carmaker's negotiating platform.

Some financial analysts had already determined that what Fiat was offering was a very bad deal for Chrysler. "The steal of the century," Forbes columnist Jerry Flint wrote of the deal in January of 2009, "Fiat gets Chrysler for next to no money, and American taxpayers must throw in $7 billion to make it happen."

By most accounts, Chrysler was in real trouble no matter what, but by announcing to the world that Chrysler had no other alternatives, Obama effectively told Fiat that Chrysler had to accept whatever they offered, eliminating Chrysler's ability to cut a better deal. That raises the question: why didn't Fiat have to make any "sacrifices," Mr. Obama?[57]

Why would Obama undercut a US company, involved in a heated negotiation, in favor of a foreign company's interest? Clear answers are not available, but at the time, there was one very curious shareholder in Fiat that raises some interesting questions. The African nation of Libya owned at least a 2 to 3 percent stake in Fiat and thus made Muammar Qaddafi (now deceased) —who at the time controlled the wealth of Libya—a direct beneficiary of a deal favoring Fiat.

The economist Ikenson explains the crippling, long-term re-percussions of Obama's actions: "The administration's willing-ness to insulate important political allies, like the UAW, from the consequences of their decisions, to shift possession of assets from shareholders and debt-holders to pensioners, and to deny 'deficiency' claims to creditors who were short-changed, will make it more difficult for companies in politically important industries to borrow from private sources when they are in trouble, thereby increasing their reliance on the government purse." In short, Obama seems to be creating the type of economy he desires, that is, one in which Washington is in control and ultimately decides which companies succeed and which ones fail.

Apparently, justice will follow on the same track. Despite his promises to "crack down" on financial crimes, Obama isn't "standing with the little people" on what appears to be the very type of fraudulent activity he promised to end. In April 2010, news broke that the Securities Exchange Commission was suing the Wall Street bank of Goldman Sachs. However, conspicuously absent was an announcement from the Department of Justice that anyone would be indicted. How curious. Obama has relentlessly attacked big business and Wall Street greed, draining every last metaphor from the leftist's lexicon used to attack Capitalism. The SEC has accused Goldman Sachs of some pretty nasty stuff, according to the *Washington Post* "The suit asserts that Goldman defrauded investors when it sold them a subprime-mortgage investment in 2007 that was secretly designed to lose value. The agency alleges that Goldman created and marketed the investment without telling its clients that Paulson & Co., a prominent hedge fund, had helped the bank assemble the investment while at the same time was placing bets that it would lose value. The bank received $15 million from Paulson & Co. for its services."

This case sounds like a test designed in purgatory to prove the mettle of a devout populist. But instead of going after Goldman Sachs like he did the Chrysler bondholders, who hadn't been accused of any wrongdoing, Obama wanted no part of a criminal investigation of his biggest donor. There could be other problems for the Obama administration as well. Treasury Secretary Timothy Geithner is notoriously close to many top Goldman officials. In fact, prior to his confirmation, Geithner's critics were on record with what they saw as conflicts of interest. In January 2009, financial risk analyst Chris Whalen told Yahoo Finance, "Geithner is the wrong man for the job because of his decision-making as President of the New York Fed. I believe Tim Geithner only represents part of Wall Street—Goldman Sachs."

Indeed, Geithner was one of the architects of the Troubled Asset Relief Program, and during that time had an unusual number of contacts with Robert Rubin, a former co-chairman of Goldman Sachs. And it was Geithner's decision to bail out American Insurance Group, a controversial move that made Goldman whole at a time when other banks such as Bear Stearns were left struggling or allowed to fail.

Obama faces potential peril if the SEC lawsuit ends up being a prosecution. But confident he has nothing to fear from his Attorney General, he displays his usual hubris by politicizing the affair to his own benefit. With staggering irony, he used the Goldman revelations to declare that this is why congress should pass his Wall Street reform bill in 2010.

Obama used the Goldman Sachs case to set a trap for Republicans, hoping that Republicans would do exactly what they ended up doing, which was to defend Goldman, a heavy contributor to the Democrats. What a deal for Obama—he collects millions and then Republicans foolishly defend his unpopular contributor, giving Obama a win-win situation: he gets the money and gets to strike the popular anti-Wall Street pose, as though he's a man of the people. Republicans could have fought back by demanding a special prosecutor to get to the bottom of this matter that the SEC calls "fraud," and should have taken it a step further by demanding the investigation include political donations and influence peddling. This is critical, considering the amount of taxpayer money used to bail out the politically connected firms.

The political fallout for Obama could have been devastating, after he publically chastised the Supreme Court for a decision that he says would allow big business more freedom to influence elections. If so, Obama would then be forced to defend himself for taking nearly one million dollars from a big bank that, according to critics, should have been indicted, while Republicans took the high road and lectured Democrats about the evils of government intervention of big banks, Wall Street and made their tainted campaign donations an issue. This incident merely validates the problems with Obama's economic worldview. It ends up being a protection racket run by politicians elected with donations from the people they claim to be policing. Goldman pays, and Obama's Justice Department looks the other way. This is why the principles of a free market are a far more honest way of doing business than government imposition of massive regulations that favors large, dishonest enterprises over small, honest ones. How else to explain the disparity of treatment between the earnest negotiations on behalf of the bondholders of Chrysler and the "fat cat bankers," as Obama would call them, of Goldman Sachs?

Amidst Obama's anti-Wall Street bluster there were always "fat cats" that could rent his friendship and support. On March 31, 2009, Republican Jim Tedisco conceded the race for the 20th district in New York to Wall Street Democrat Scott Murphy after counting some of the absentee ballots in a special election. After the lead changed hands several times during the month of March, Murphy was leading by a few hundred votes out of over 155,000 ballots cast. Tedisco conceded with class compared to the way Democrats handle such matters. If Democrats are behind by a small percentage of votes, they automatically assume they can find that number of votes one way or another. Oftentimes that means finding bags full of ballots in the trunks of cars, or attempting to disqualify absentee votes cast by members of the military. There is nothing sacrosanct to a Democrat seeking power. That is why in many elections around the country Republicans must win by a theft proof margin. It is a safe bet that if Murphy, the Democrat, had been down by the number of votes that triggered Tedisco's concession, the 20th district would have been swarming with lawyers claiming vote fraud and accusing Tedisco of stealing the election. Their fellow Democrats in the press corps would have done their part and dutifully reported whatever the leftist politicians needed them to say to legitimize their effort.

Obama quickly tried to claim the special election as some kind of victory for himself. Obama said Murphy "courageously championed the economic plans we need to lift our nation and put it on a better path. And he will continue to do so in Congress." One of those "economic plans" was Obama's nearly $1 trillion spending bill. Even though Murphy had not been elected when the stimulus came up for a vote, he had announced that he supported it during the campaign. Obama's "stimulus bill" contained a bailout for insurance giant American Insurance Group (AIG), including the highly controversial bonuses for AIG executives.

Obama had just spent the previous two years on a campaign to blame all of the world's problems on President Bush, capitalism, free enterprise, and the war on terror. But now, after finding out that his administration's deal to bail out American Insurance Group (AIG) —including massive bonuses to AIG executives— was extremely unpopular, the hunt for a scapegoat became priority No. 1. Obama said it wasn't his fault that no one wanted to take the blame for what came to be known as "bonus-gate."

By that time, Americans were waking up. They were realizing that nebulous campaign slogans really don't fix anything, and Obama's approval ratings began to sink making the Tedisco— Murphy special election that much more important. At that point, it was like the "prove it" shot in the basketball game "around-the-world" —Obama needed it to validate that his election wasn't a fluke.

The facts staring back at Obama were that just five months earlier, the very same district gave Democrat Kirsten Gillibrand a twenty-four point margin of victory. Then just three months into Obama's presidency, in an unusually high turnout for a special election, it ended in a statistical dead heat. Interestingly, Obama stayed out of the race fearing a Murphy loss would be seen as a referendum against his presidency. But on the day before the election when Obama saw that Murphy had a steady eight point surge in the polls, and what looked like a decisive margin for Murphy, he jumped in with a last minute endorsement—and the White House, through the back door, was selling this through their surrogates in the press as a referendum on his presidency. Then when it ended in a tie, suggesting a dramatic rebuke of Obama, his friends in the media dropped the whole referendum conceit. If it had been a clear Murphy win, the media would have boasted about how popular Obama was and that the Democrats were unstoppable.

The thick irony of that special election was that Democrat Scott Murphy was the personification of what the Democratic Party says is wrong with the country. He was a Wall Street financier; he had outsourced jobs to India; he lived well and paid himself and his top executives big bonuses. He was a real life Gordon Gekko. Let me be clear, I absolutely support capitalism and free market economics—but the Democrats don't. If Murphy had been a Republican, Democrats and the press would have savaged him for his big business background—he couldn't have gotten elected dogcatcher. But, as we have seen too many times before, liberals are duplicitous. During the campaign, one of the New York papers called me for an interview to discuss the candidates, and when I mentioned Murphy's background to the reporter he asked, "What do you have against rich people?" I told him I have nothing against business people who do well for themselves, but these are the very people that Democrats tell us are what is wrong with America. This is about Democrats creating straw men and teaching their base to hate capitalists, and then being hypocritical enough to run one for office. If capitalists are evil, which they are in the Democrats worldview, then why wasn't Scott Murphy?

In the end, the special election in New York District 20 was less about the two people running and more about voters concern for their country and what Obama's policies would mean for the future. It telegraphed what was to come a year and a half later in the 2010 midterm election. That is why a 24-point Democrat advantage in November 2008 was reversed—it was a clear message to Obama. But over 3 years later, he still hadn't gotten it. The arrogance of power had desensitized him to such an obvious outcry.

Chapter 12

Vote Right or Die

In March 2010, President Obama finally passed his massive health-care bill. Although the exact staggering cost to the American people has yet to be determined, the attendant increase in taxes and misery, as well as a corresponding decline in quality and standards, will most likely remain unquantifiable for many years to come. But one thing is sure—he accomplished something that Democrats had been trying to do and failing at for more than half a century. So, it was comically ironic that Democrats running for reelection in 2010 wanted to talk about almost anything but healthcare.

Democrats were so wary of being seen in the same state, much less the same room as Obama, they went to the bench and brought out accused rapist and former President Bill Clinton to campaign for them. Clinton, who was credibly accused of raping Juanita Broddrick, apparently wielded much greater star power among Democrats than Obama did.

It was just back in the early days of 2010 that Bill Clinton addressed the entire Democratic caucus on Capitol Hill to discuss then-post-Scott Brown-election, and the stalled tax and regulation package known as the "health insurance reform bill." Although he failed spectacularly during his own presidency to pass an even less ambitious package of socialist engineering, Clinton is widely regarded in the mainstream media as a "health care expert." He focused not on the merits of the bill—in fact he said the details were unimportant—but instead focused on the politics of not passing anything. That, he said, would be the killer; if Democrats didn't pass healthcare reform they would be perceived as a "do nothing Congress." His subsequent advice to Democrats—pass it now, fix it later if you must—came with an ominous prediction: don't pass it, and you'll face a tough reelection bid this fall. In light of the circumstances of that election, Democrats might want to rethink taking advice from Clinton. Like many a Clinton audience before them, these Democrats failed to discern the hidden message Bill was really sending: this is my long-term plan to reclaim relevance.

It was strange to see Democrats try to resuscitate their party by attacking regular Americans who have been compelled to run for office with a man who was not only accused of rape, but who sold national security secrets to Communist China, contributed substantially to the mortgage crisis, erected the information wall between the FBI and the CIA (that many credit with America's inability to predict or prevent the terrorist attacks of 9/11), and cheated on his income taxes when he and his wife were rich. Khalid Sheik Mohammed must have turned them down.

"And of course they got the wrestling federation lady in Connecticut and the witchcraft lady in Delaware and, I tell you, so far they've gathered up about everybody for this Tea Party but the Mad Hatter and Alice in Wonderland. I'll give it to them," Clinton said in his standard disingenuous fashion at a fundraising event back in 2010. That was back when Democrats still thought it was "real cool" to mock and ridicule the Tea Parties. Of course, that was hardly the first time that Clinton had verbally assaulted the Tea Partiers. In 2009 he used the nastier sexual slur, "tea baggers," referring to Americans who deign to exercise their First Amendment rights in public. Not too surprising coming from a bona fide scumbagger like Bill Clinton.

The way Democrats attacked Christine O'Donnell for a tardy mortgage payment, you would never have imagined that Barbara Boxer was one of them. The Democrats and their propaganda team, also known as the mainstream media, surely hoped that no one would recall that Boxer wrote 143 bad checks on the House of Representatives bank while she was a member of Congress. Is it possible that Democrats considered O'Donnell's personal finances too pristine to serve in the US Senate?

Democrats were desperate going into the midterm election, but they had no idea how severe their losses would be. Then came Speaker of the House Nancy Pelosi's statement "we have to pass the bill so you can find out what is in it"—the arrogance and condescension in that one line became the allegory for all that was wrong with the political class in Washington. Several Republican legislators dutifully reported disturbing elements about the contents of the health-care bill, even as the reigning Democrats in the House of Representatives played bait-and-switch with what ended up in the final bill. But no one confronted the President about his many bold lies about health insurance in the United States.

From 2009 to 2010, during his year-long pitch for his so-called "health insurance reform," President Obama repeatedly exaggerated problems, obfuscated facts, and manufactured lies about the condition of health care and health insurance in America. It was all part of a conscious and calculated effort to sow fear among the populace, if not exactly the "politics as usual" that he derides at every opportunity, then certainly something even more sinister.

In a 2010 speech at George Mason University, President Obama told a captive crowd that health-care reform will henceforth mean insurance companies can't cancel an insured's coverage when they have a claim. "This year, they will be banned from dropping your coverage when you get sick. Those practices will end," he declared.

Obama repeated that sentiment hundreds, if not thousands, of times—and it was an outright lie. According to attorney Richard Giller, a leading expert on insurance coverage, before Obama's healthcare bill was passed, it was illegal in all fifty American states to cancel an insured's coverage for getting sick. In fact, I spoke with an actuary for a state insurance commission. Requesting anonymity, the government actuary stated unequivocally that Obama's claim was completely untrue. "These policies cannot be cancelled. They are guaranteed renewable and have been for over twenty years," he said referring to health insurance policies. "Guaranteed renewable" means the insurance company cannot cancel the coverage for any reason except nonpayment of premiums.

President Obama wove his Americans-are-pathetic-victims narrative with abandon: "They will continue to jack up premiums 40 percent or 50 percent or 60 percent, as they have in the last few weeks, without any accountability whatsoever," he said in his speech at George Mason.

Mr. Giller informed me that in more than half the states, insurance companies were strictly accountable to the government of the state in which they operate, forbidden from raising rates without specific approval. Furthermore, insurance companies are barred from raising one person's health insurance policy premium without first raising the premium for the entire underwriting category to which that person belongs. Additionally, "most states review all rate increases according to the loss ratio standards," (which means that the state not only reviews to make sure the rate is not too high, but also to ensure that the rate is high enough to pay the expected claims), confirms this government actuary.

"Because if this vote fails, the insurance industry will continue to run wild in America," Obama said. But in reality, the insurance industry is among the most regulated business sectors in America. The only industry "running wild" in this country at that time was the big government industry of the Democrats in Washington, so intoxicated with power, so consumed with their own importance, so recklessly devoted to their far left agenda that they believed they were accountable to no one. The voters changed that the first chance they got after the passage of the healthcare bill, but very few in the press corps had the temerity to request supportive evidence of their outlandish claims beforehand.

Obama also accused insurance companies of doing what he, then Speaker Pelosi and Senate Majority Leader Harry Reid had been doing all along—engaging in fear-mongering. "That's why their lobbyists are stalking the halls of Congress as we speak. That's why they're pouring millions of dollars into negative ads. That's why they're doing everything they can to kill this bill." No, they weren't. This health-care bill forced millions of people to buy health insurance from the very companies Obama said didn't want the bill to pass. Obama had adopted the use of the straw man fallacy and used it to push for nearly every piece of legislation he wanted.

Among the other outrageous claims made by Obama was that there was half a trillion dollars lost in "waste, fraud and abuse" of Medicare. But if there really is half a trillion dollars of waste, fraud and abuse in Medicare, why hadn't Obama identified it and used those funds to jumpstart the economy instead of the piles of taxpayer cash that were consumed by his failed stimulus bill?

Some estimates indicate that Obama's health-care bill includes funding for over sixteen thousand new Internal Revenue Service agents to enforce compliance with its complex regulations. That seems a bit strange for something that Democrats claimed most Americans wanted. If Americans really needed his brand of "health-care reform," why does Obama think he would need the IRS to enforce it? After the healthcare bill passed, Obama spent millions more in taxpayer dollars touring the country in an attempt to convince us just how lucky we were that he managed to get his bill through Congress.

Any health care plan will have winners and losers. That is a fact. Under the Obama plan healthcare will be distributed more evenly maybe, which sounds nice in theory, however, in reality this means that some Americans will see their current level of healthcare decrease. The only way to provide care to more people with the same or less money is to pick losers.

In August 2009, during one of Obama's staged town hall meetings on health care, a woman with cancer and no healthcare coverage asked a prewritten question and received a staged hug after Obama told her that he would help her. It was no surprise to find out she was an Obama campaign worker. The snake oil salesmen of the nineteenth century used to seed their audiences with shills to talk up their cure, too.

This deceptive practice was a charade used to imply that under Obama's plan the insurance-less woman would have her cancer cured. Americans didn't fall for it though, mainly because they were watching what Obama was doing instead of believing what he was saying. But occasionally Obama did go off script and reveal the true nature of his healthcare plan. Such was the case in a June 2009 healthcare town hall styled meeting when the daughter of an elderly woman asked if her mother's will to live would be considered when needing medical care. Obama's revealing response was: "Maybe you're better off not having the surgery, but taking the painkiller."

Obama's message was clear. Some people do not get access because the government underwriters callously determine that saving their lives will cost too much. Many in the liberal media wailed that this interpretation of Obama's words was unfair. But Obama's Special Healthcare Advisor Dr. Ezekiel Emanuel makes pretty clear where Obama is headed with his idea of how healthcare should work: "Because none of the currently used systems satisfy all ethical requirements for just allocation, we propose an alternative: the complete lives system. This system incorporates five principles: youngest-first, prognosis, save the most lives, lottery, and instrumental value. As such, it prioritizes younger people who have not yet lived a complete life and will be unlikely to do so without aid. Many thinkers have accepted complete lives as the appropriate focus of distributive justice: 'individual human lives, rather than individual experiences, [are] the units over which any distributive principle should operate.' Although there are important differences between these thinkers, they share a core commitment to consider entire lives rather than events or episodes, which is also the defining feature of the complete lives system."[58]

One of the most interesting things about Emanuel's writing is how hard it is to find it on the internet. Searches for it mostly turn up media reports and liberal websites that accuse "the right wing" of distorting and twisting Obama's healthcare advisor's words. So let me be clear: The passage above is taken directly from the British medical journal The Lancet, dated January 31, 2009. Ezekiel Emanuel (and two others) authored this journal entry, and it is a clear and obvious protocol for managing healthcare and ranks healthcare recipients by priority according to value to society. The use of the phrase "distributive justice" seems to fit Obama's world view in everything else, so why is it so hard for the left to accept that he sees healthcare in the same way?

In 2010, Grace-Marie Turner of the Galen Institute published an analysis of the "six worst flaws" of the Obama healthcare plan. Among them, "...a uniform, government-defined benefits package. Rather than letting individuals pick plans based on their own needs, the Obama proposal requires insurers to offer a minimum benefits package. Congress will soon see every special interest group—from alcohol-abuse counselors to chiropractors and acupuncturists—lining up on Capitol Hill lobbying to have its service included in the 'minimum' package."[59] Do not be fooled; the rationing of care will form the bedrock of the government plan.

Just look at Medicare. The government, not doctors, determine what the cost value is for a particular procedure, Diagnostic Related Groupings as they are called, and the government dictates the treatment protocols and how much the doctor can charge for any procedure, as well as how long a patient is allowed to stay in the hospital for each procedure. This should make everyone question the potential dangers of further government intervention into the healthcare industry.

In June 2009, the *New York Times* reported that a *Times/CBS* poll determined that "most Americans would be willing to pay higher taxes so everyone could have health insurance and that they said the government could do a better job of holding down health-care costs than the private sector."[60] The results of the 2010 elections raise serious questions about the *New York Times* ability to conduct a poll. The poll question that would be more relevant is: How many of those polled actually pay taxes? It is easy to say you are in favor of higher taxes for more benefits when you are not the one paying the higher taxes. But there it is again, Obama and the Democrats' economic philosophy, which is the takers decide how much the payers should give them.

The reality is this: There will always be some people who receive less care than others under any healthcare system. Under the free market it is those who take from the system who get less care than those who pay for the system; under Obama's plan the government sets standards to determine who gets care. This is especially alarming considering the way Obama has used the power of government to allocate resources to reward his supporters and punish those who supported his opposition. No one should be comfortable with a system that gives the power of life and death to a politically appointed bureaucrat, especially one with easy access through public documents to information on whom the patient supported.

The Obama Administration and the Democrat controlled Congress rammed the healthcare bill through Congress before the American people had a chance to understand its devastating ramifications. The *Wall Street Journal* once opined, "The more we inspect the House bill, the more it looks to be one of the worst pieces of legislation ever introduced in Congress." Sadly, few members of Congress actually read bills before voting on them.

Part IV

The Media, Democrats, Obama and the Prestige of Cruelty

Chapter 13

Poll Rigging

In early April 2009, as tea parties were sprouting and America was becoming disenchanted with Obama, the liberal news media tried to throw him a lifeline. CBS reported on a *CBS/New York Times* poll that showed irrational exuberance from the American people over Obama, but a closer look revealed what skeptics already suspected.

"Mr. Obama's overall approval rating, meanwhile, has hit a new high of 66 percent, up from 64 percent last month. His disapproval rating stands at 24 percent," boasted a press release from either *CBS News* or the Obama campaign, which is a difference without much distinction. According to former Democratic pollster Patrick Caddell, "there is a problem" with the way the poll was conducted.

"Their poll of all adults shows an extreme Democratic edge on party preference of 16 points... I know of no other public poll that has such an extreme partisan gap," says Caddell, once considered a star in Democratic Party circles until his insistence on honesty with the American people put him at odds with the Democrat Party leadership.

In other words, it appears The *New York Times* and CBS *"News"* cooked the poll numbers by scrounging around until they found enough people who agreed with their editors' opinions about Obama. Caddell says, "The original raw sample already showed a partisan difference of 8.5 percent but "when weighting or 'adjusting' the numbers the partisan gap went over 16 points.

In effect what they did was reduce the Republicans in the sample by 13 percent and increased the number of Democrats by 12 percent. Particularly strange was the number of Independent voters was only changed 2 percent."

Caddell accuses the *Times* and *CBS* of being guilty of either one of two things: "It is either terrible methodology or the Bernie Madoff school of polling. Small demographic adjustments are ordinary, but these extremes are unprecedented."

CBS used the same poll to proclaim, "67 percent say world leaders respect Mr. Obama, while 18 percent say they do not respect the president. That's a sharp contrast to the response when this question was asked about Mr. Obama's predecessor, George W. Bush, in July 2006: Just 30 percent then said the president is respected by the leaders of other countries."

"Respect" is an odd choice of words considering immediately after being elected Obama stood on European soil—that is stained with the blood of American soldiers—and apologized for American arrogance. The only apology Obama owes is the one to America for his own arrogance. On the other hand, a Pew Research poll conducted in March of 2009, just before the New York Times/CBS poll, showed the new president in a different light: "For all of his hopes about bipartisanship, Barack Obama has the most polarized early job approval ratings of any president in the past four decades."[61] Unsurprisingly, most people didn't hear about the Pew study; it would have been too difficult for the media to paint Obama as an adored leader if people knew how different the reality was.

During the process of investigating media polling bias, I discovered a very troubling relationship between the Associated Press, its polling firm GfK, and the federal government. The Associated Press has failed to reveal the startling fact that its polling firm, GfK, has been granted federal government contracts since Obama has been in office. The news may not surprise the many skeptics of the liberal media because they have come to expect this sort of bias from mainstream press outlets, but this goes beyond bias-as-usual and well into a dangerous area of the government purchase of favorable news coverage, and as you are about to see, a crime against transparency. By using polls to invent favorable news for Obama, the AP has helped create the impression that Obama's reelection is inevitable, and is essentially pushing his campaign strategy for him.

In late February 2012, the AP reported that their polling firm had determined that Obama would beat any of the Republican candidates in a head to head matchup. A closer look at the raw polling data reveals that the AP and GfK had used faulty data to compile the numbers by sampling ten percent more Democrat/Democrat leaning than Republican/Republican leaning respondents. This is faulty polling as nearly all national polls have determined that there is now an even split between Republican and Democrat populations. And the results of properly calibrated polls are strikingly different. For example, a Gallup poll taken at roughly the same time as the AP poll was taken showed Republican Mitt Romney with a four point advantage over Obama, and then Republican contender Rick Santorum in a dead heat with the President.

For the AP, which, like the other mainstream media outlets, has made an issue of demanding disclosure from candidates about their political donors in the name of "transparency" this duplicity must be scrutinized. This is a news agency getting apparent special treatment from the government while skewing political news coverage to benefit the Obama administration, which controls the purse strings for at least part of their polling firm's business. I began investigating this obvious conflict of interest in May of 2011 after noticing the unusual financial relationship between the newswire service, its polling firm GfK, and the federal government—and prima facie evidence that the relationship had influenced the AP's reporting on the Obama administration.

A May 11, 2011 AP report promoted the idea that President Obama's re-election was a foregone conclusion based on a poll conducted by its partner firm GfK. Just two months earlier GfK had announced that it had received clearance for federal government contracts to do marketing and research for US government agencies. Closer examination revealed that the May 11th AP report based its conclusions on a severely flawed polling model that provided a significant advantage to President Obama in calculating his favorability ratings on a number of issues from national security to the economy.

The flawed polling data influenced other media including *ABC News*, *Time*, the *Washington Post* and *Yahoo News* which ran the AP's reportage without scrutiny. The following is from the May 11, 2011 news report and was not labeled commentary: "President Barack Obama's approval rating has hit its highest point in two years—60 percent—and more than half of Americans now say he deserves to be re-elected, according to an Associated Press-GFK poll taken after U.S. forces killed al-Qaida leader Osama bin Laden...Comfortable majorities of the public now call Obama a strong leader who will keep America safe. Nearly three-fourths—73 percent—also now say they are confident that Obama can effectively handle terrorist threats."[62]

There was no downside for Obama mentioned in the "news" story authored by Lis Sidoti and Jennifer Agiesta. Neither is there any mention that GfK, the Associated Press partner and the polling firm that conducted this survey, had been approved, two months prior, for a major contract with the federal government. In a press release dated March 1, 2011 GFK revealed the following: "GfK Custom Research North America, an industry leader in innovative market research tools and services, today announced that it has been awarded the General Services Administration (GSA) Mission Oriented Business Integrated Services contract (MOBIS). Having this contract allows GfK to directly and seamlessly serve public sector clients. As the primary purchasing agent for most US governmental agencies, having the GSA validation signifies that GfK meets the high standards to enable government agencies to easily do business with GfK through various contract vehicles."

According to the AP, "The Associated Press and GfK launched a polling partnership in September 2008." According to an analysis by Tom Blumer at Pajamas Media, "AP reporters didn't ... tell readers how 'skewed' May's poll was. Forty-six percent of those surveyed identified themselves as Democrats, 29 percent as Republicans, and 4 percent as independents (after classifying leaners); 20 percent didn't know. By contrast, the latest available party identification results from Rasmussen as of April have the GOP at 34.8 percent, Dems at 33.5 percent, and 31.7% as not affiliated. Gallup, in an aggregate of 21 separate polls conducted last year, shows a Democrat-Republican split of 45 percent – 44 percent."

Since nearly all major polling firms consider the Democrat-to-Republican ratio of voters to be virtually even in number, AP/GfK's statistical model of 46% sampling of Democrats and 29 percent Republican would give the appearance of significant advantage in the outcome to a Democrat, in this case Barack Obama.

The author of the tainted story from last May, Liz Sidoti, refused to comment after repeated attempts to allow her the opportunity to defend her reporting. The AP's reportage was once considered the gold standard of journalism; today it is the tool of a corrupt administration. The AP had been politicizing the news leftward for some time, but Barack Obama's nomination to run for president in 2008 seemed to bring out the worst in slanted coverage. An example of just how far the AP was willing to go in order to throw the election to Obama was when in October of 2008 it attempted to level the playing field for Obama by excusing his associations with hippie-radical William Ayers with an assertion that McCain had a connection with Iran/Contra.

This feeble attack relied on the imputed allegation that any association with the Nicaraguan freedom fighters, known as the Contras, is inherently bad. McCain's "link" was based on his position on the advisory board of Gen. John Singlaub's U.S. Council for World Freedom. That organization supported efforts to provide aid to the Contras, but had nothing to do with Iran.

In his lead to the AP story, Pete Yost wrote, "Barack Obama has his William Ayers connection. Now John McCain may have an Iran-Contra connection. In the 1980s, McCain served on the advisory board to the U.S. chapter of an international group linked to ultra-right-wing death squads in Central America." Lest anyone forget, during the Cold War, the liberal media defined anyone fighting communism as a "right-wing death squad."

The AP report states, "McCain's tie to Singlaub's council is undergoing renewed scrutiny after his campaign criticized Obama for his link to Ayers, a former radical who engaged in violent acts 40 years ago."[63] The AP's basis for comparison between Ayers and Singlaub is outrageous and sleazy. A true comparison of

Ayers and Singlaub would point out that Ayers violently attacked his own country and countrymen, whereas Singlaub risked his life numerous times to defend his country and serve his fellow Americans. If a man can be judged by the company he keeps, Obama's ties to Ayers indicate rebellious hatred and violence; McCain's ties to Singlaub indicate honor, duty, and sacrifice.

The most damnable statement in Yost's article is his nonsensical association of Singlaub with Nazis. Yost stated, "The council created by retired Army Maj. Gen. John Singlaub was the U.S. chapter of the World Anti-Communist League, an international organization linked to former Nazi collaborators."[64] To make it clear, perhaps Mr. Yost should be reminded that Singlaub was shot fighting the Nazis in World War II and devoted his entire life to the cause of freedom. It is inexcusable for Yost to besmirch the reputation of such an honorable man under any circumstances, but even worse when used as a dirty political trick, to help take the focus off of another candidate that deserved more scrutiny, not less, and all done under the guise of unbiased journalism.

Making Yost's comments even more ridiculous, the AP's reporting on this was not even original. It turns out they lifted it, inaccuracies and all, from an anti-American website where it had appeared two days earlier. To make matters worse, the AP had all but declared their candidate of choice when they dismissed former Gov. Sarah Palin's remarks about Obama's links to Ayers as "unsubstantiated." Actually, Palin's remarks about the Obama-Ayers links were far more substantiated than the AP's wispy attacks on McCain's "links" to "right-wing death squads." In fact, they provided no evidence at all to back up their vicious claim that the U.S. Council for World Freedom was linked to "right-wing death squads" or Nazis.

The story has such a strange paradox because it is Obama who is linked to controversial figures whose agendas are more akin to that of the Nazis. Rashid Khalidi, a longtime associate and friend of Obama, and Robert Malley, who once served on Obama's campaign, both have associations with the terrorist group Hamas, which has a stated agenda that includes the annihilation of the Jews. It is Obama himself who had already made it known at that time that he had no reservations about negotiating with Iranian President Mahmoud Ahmadinejad, who has vowed to wipe Israel off the map. The disgusting bias in the AP's reporting can only be labeled outright propaganda.

Obama's coterie of sycophants, many which belong to the press corps, have been at war with anyone who disagrees with Obama's agenda or questions his background or motives. The worst vitriol has been aimed at the Tea Party movement. *Fox News Channel*'s Bill O'Reilly usually defended the Tea Partiers and treated their cause fairly, but at times even O'Reilly may have been influenced by the leftist media. On his February 16, 2010 broadcast, following the publication of a *New York Times* article, O'Reilly asked Sarah Palin this question: "Do you think the birther people should have a place at the Tea Party table...Do you see the danger if that becomes the headline...?" The danger of the "birther" question is irrelevant because the Democrat Party apologist *Times* will always find something that they can use to try and discredit the Left's opposition. If there is a crowd of a thousand tea party protesters, the media will canvas all of them until they find one willing to say something objectionable. But there is a new and growing understanding of the media that has diminished their capacity to do damage to conservatives. That understanding means that when the *Times* or any of the elite media attack regular Americans, Tea Partiers or otherwise, it doesn't harm the people they attack—as much as it further marginalizes the liberal media.

The *Times* article in question, from February 2010, was almost a parody itself. It was thick with drama about angry people being drawn into conspiracy theories that the *Times* said had been long ago discredited. "Urged on by conservative commentators, waves of newly minted activists are turning to once-obscure books and Web sites and discovering a set of ideas long dismissed as the preserve of conspiracy theorists... In this view, Mr. Obama and many of his predecessors (including George W. Bush) have deliberately undermined the Constitution and free enterprise for the benefit of a shadowy international network of wealthy elites," stated the *Times*.[65]

Of course, George Soros, billionaire financier from Europe who has spent tens of millions of dollars getting Democrats elected here, objected to being called "a shadowy wealthy elite," but Italian automaker Fiat didn't mind it so much. If the Tea Partiers had, in fact, said they believed our government was supporting an "international network of elites" they would have scooped the *New York Times*. The December 28, 2011 *Wall Street Journal Online* reported the following: "America's central bank, the Federal Reserve, is engaged in a bailout of European banks. Surprisingly, its operation is largely unnoticed here."[66]

Among the other conspiracy theories the *Times* said were long ago dismissed was the theory that if liberals could, they would elect a president with links to Marxist terror groups such as the Weather Underground and its founder Williams Ayers or an admitted Communist such as Van Jones or a disciple of Saul Alinsky. The *Times* assures us that those conspiracy theorists are way off base.

The *Times* also warned that the Tea Party participants could prove potentially violent. The *Times* quoted left-wing, so-called "civil rights activist" Tony Stewart saying: "When people start wearing guns to rallies, what's the next thing that happens?"[67] Over three years later we are still waiting for the first victim of a violent Tea Partier; but in the meantime, Harvard graduate, liberal elitist and enthusiastic Obama supporter Amy Bishop shot and killed three of her unarmed colleagues at the University of Alabama at about the same time as the *Times* was labeling Tea Partiers as dangerous. And wasn't Unabomber Ted Kaczynski one of theirs too? Perhaps the liberal media should be investigating the dangerous left-wing militias, or as they like to call themselves, "community organizers," "labor unions," and "environmentalists."

The *Times* sees a potential takeover of the Republican Party: "tense struggles have erupted over whether the Republican apparatus will co-opt these new coalitions or vice versa."[68] The "tense struggles" for the Democratic Party were won by sixties radicals, but to point that out makes you a conspiracy theorist according to the *Times* and other mainstream media outlets, even when the Democrats publically acknowledge their extremism—such as when they embraced the Occupy Wall Street protesters.

Americans saw the media drive the election of Barack Obama with nary a scintilla of investigation into his background, experience or who shaped the way he thinks or how he might govern. The very same media that spent years investigating George W. Bush's early 1970's military record. And when these so-called journalists could find nothing damaging in Bush's military record, they simply used faked documents at a critical time before the 2004 election to try and throw the election to John Kerry who was trying to run on a war record he did not own, but received no media scrutiny. These are some of the reasons why loose coalitions of Americans began meeting peacefully to try and figure out what has happened to their country.

I spent years as an investigative journalist and I have no conspiracy theories about the media; but I do have an explanation for why so many distrust the news from elite media outlets. By ignoring Obama's past and the radical things he has done as President, from his appointments to the massive spending and "redistribution" schemes, the liberal so-called mainstream media have provoked the very conspiracy theories that they now mock. So now we are left with a broken government and an angry, cynical people—and the very elites who broke it are mocking the people for no longer trusting them.

The shocking mass murder visited upon Tucson in January 2011 by a lunatic loner provided the Democrats and the media with another opportunity to show that they haven't a shred of decency. The Associated Press led the yellow hoard with minute-by-minute accusations before the victims of this horrific tragedy were even evacuated to the hospital. The media coverage went something like this: "Most people believe there is a Tea Party and Sarah Palin connection to all of this." That was before the name of the shooter was even known.

Follow-up reports operated along a similar narrative: "What is this Loughner's connection to the Tea Party? Has he ever been to a Tea Party? Does he know anybody that ever went to a Tea Party? Does he have a 'T' in his name? Were they selling tea in the store where the shooting took place? We have our suspects—anyone who thinks the government is spending too much!" Tragically, that account was only slightly hyperbolic.

Days later, and with stunning chutzpah, the Democrats who have been calling people associated with Tea Parties every vicious name you can think of, like "terrorist," and saying that they are "dangerous" and "un-American", "thugs" and "brown shirts"— were telling us that we need to have "a more civil tone" when addressing them. This is rather hypocritical coming from the Party whose leader referred to us as their "enemies." And like the increasingly disconnected royal aspirants the political class has become, they demean us as brutes and then demand that we pay so they can be protected from us.

There is no event too tragic for Democrats and their allies in the media to exploit for political advantage. It was obvious to everyone that this was a naked attempt to silence all criticism of the left-wing establishment while it finished off its "fundamental transformation of America." The very left-wingers who have been tearing this country apart, using the most inflammatory rhetoric to attack peaceful American Tea Party protesters who are trying to save the country, were accusing their victims of being dangerous and inspiring the violence in Tucson. Left-wing absurdist David Brock was on *MSNBC* following Obama's civility speech in Tucson, still on the attack. "Glenn Beck himself has been responsible for three thwarted assassination attempts this year," Brock said.

Any reasonable person knew that there was no evidence linking Jared Loughner to Palin or any Tea Party group. If the same standards were applied to Democrats that have been applied to Tea Partiers, Democrat Senator Dick Durbin would be held responsible for Nidal Hasan's murderous rampage at Fort Hood, Texas. Durbin compared American soldiers to Nazis on the floor of the US Senate. If the Left wants to link the crosshairs of a political campaign to Tea Party groups and Sarah Palin, then what Dick Durbin said was tantamount to deputizing Hasan for his murderous act of terrorism.

What is even more absurd is that Durbin and his colleague in the Senate, John Kerry, were two of the first out of the box to demand civility. Does anyone remember Kerry's remark during the George H. W. Bush administration that the Secret Service should "shoot Quayle" (referring to then-Vice President Dan Quayle) in the event that President Bush was shot?

Speaking of "targeting" people, has anyone noticed that the state government of Pennsylvania, run by a Democrat, has a television ad that targets its own citizens? "Your name is Tom. Nice car, Tom. Nice house," a voice says, as the video image of a "target" with a bull's-eye focuses in on a house, warning that "Tom" better pay his taxes because, as the ad warns its viewers, "we know where you live." That ad received national attention in 2010, and yet, there was no media outrage about it. But if using a target for a political opponent is "dangerous" and promotes a "climate of hate," as our liberal elites tell us, then the government putting a bull's-eye on a citizen's house qualifies as tyranny.

So, the Left claims to seize the high ground while accusing us of being accomplices to murder. Then they demand we treat them with civility. Or else. The logical conclusion to this parade of absurdities would be for Obama to appoint his former pastor, Jeremiah Wright, to be the Civility Czar.

The 2010 elections once again brought out the ugly bias of the mainstream media. These elections brought forth an influx of candidates for office who had never run before. This thoroughly angered the political class because it was a threat to their power base and they knew that if outsiders figured out how to run for office and win, the bums would be on their way out. The mainstream media hated them also, but that is because most were conservative and ran on a platform of returning to the Constitution.

Art Robinson is a decent, accomplished American, and brilliant scientist, who ran for Congress in Oregon's 4th Congressional District against liberal Congressman Peter DeFazio, an entrenched member of the liberal glitterati. Robinson probably wasn't aware, but when you take on a liberal, you take on his entire family too. That is why *MSNBC* got involved, when Robinson appeared on a show hosted by someone named Rachel Maddow. No one who is reading this book, or who can read at all for that matter, would likely know who she is, and since more people are listening in on a cordless phone conversation than have ever watched her show, it must be explained that Rachel Maddow is a pinhead. And, if anyone had ever seen her show, they'd know that—much like the rest of the hosts on *MSNBC*—her synapses are firing like peanut butter [Note to Liberals—who generally eschew both firing and peanut butter—that means SLOW].

Typically, Maddow avoids having bright people on the air; who needs spirited debate, when you can instead cull your guests from a vast and vapid pool of fellow believers? But, since Democrats and the White House were trying to gin up outrage about groups of Americans who had been pooling their resources to try and reclaim their country from the Radical Left, Maddow had Art Robinson on to try and embarrass him over some group that spent $150,000 to attack his opponent—the liberal Congressman Pete DeFazio—and thereby help elect Art Robinson.

Maddow, in all her manufactured huff over one hundred thousand dollars, looked just like the Mike Meyers' character, Dr. Evil, when he wields pinky to lip to breathlessly threaten the immediate destruction of the entire world, unless he receive the "sum of... one million dollars."

Where was the outrage when Obama raised hundreds of millions of dollars from dubious sources, including foreign donations? Another Maddow objective in interviewing Robinson was to un-debunk the manufactured, and now thoroughly discredited, man-made global warming hoax. Only the most hearty anti-corporate, anti-development, anti-progress types—and morons—buy into this silly notion anymore. It was the fool's gold of the green movement, and it's unbelievable that Maddow and the Left still cling to voodoo notions of global warming the way she likely clings to her disco shoes and leisure suits. Robinson, of course, was one of the lead scientists to debunk global warming.

What is even more outrageous is how MSNBC is attacking real Americans on behalf of an anti-American president who is trying to spread this notion that Americans taking back their country are being backed by foreign money. Laughable on the face of it, since Obama has been the best gift we have ever given the enemies of America.

Obama is out peddling this idea that "foreign interests" are backing the pro-America Tea Party movement here. He attacked Americans for Prosperity, a group backed by the Koch Brothers from Wichita, Kansas, for running ads promoting freedom; unfortunately, freedom is Obama's real enemy. This is the same Obama that, to this day, refuses to disclose his own donors from his presidential campaign. Obama refuses to disclose the source of hundreds of millions of dollars, some of which we know came from foreign sources. As anyone familiar with them knows, the Koch brothers have done far more for America than Obama has. In fact, instead of attacking them, he ought to be asking their advice about how to create some jobs.

Chapter 14

Democrats, Media, and the Two Faces of Racism

As many have known for years, and warned frequently, the Democratic Party strategy of race-baiting was merely a tactic to gain political power for their white leadership. Although it sounds really cynical, take a look at a tactic used in the 2010 election. Old habits die hard, as the saying goes. And so, too, do deeply-rooted, institutional policies reflective of a rotten core— like the Democratic Party's harboring of bold racial animus and disdain while claiming the mantle of "diversity," and at the same time employing the most overtly divisive racial political strategies seen in this country during the past sixty years.

If not for racism, how else to account for the pervasive corruption in the Democratic party, and yet, under the authority of the Democrat-controlled U.S. House of Representatives, from 2006 through 2010 election, only one white member was under investigation, while at least eight black members were?

In September 2009, Citizens for Ethics in Washington, a liberal organization named several top Democrats as corrupt, and also white. Rep. Alan B. Mollohan (D-WV), Rep. John P. Murtha (D-PA now deceased), Rep. Laura Richardson (D-CA), to name a few, and that does not include the privileges that then Speaker of the House, Nancy Pelosi rewarded herself with, such as flying her family members on Congressional junkets at taxpayer expense; and then there's Pelosi's insider credit card deal that netted her and her husband hefty sums. And yet, not one of them was investigated by the Democrat-chaired Office of Congressional Ethics.

So, what is it exactly that differentiates those members of the Democratic Party from, say, Charlie Rangel, Maxine Waters, or Jesse Jackson, Jr., all of whom enjoyed "official, enhanced scrutiny" while Democrats were in charge of the House? Here is how Democrat supporter Froma Harrop described Pelosi's strategy for the 2010 election in her *Real Clear Politics* column: "That the Democrats under the microscope—New York Rep. Charles B. Rangel and California Rep. Maxine Waters—are both black only underscores the seriousness with which the Democratic leadership supports a new set of standards for conduct."[69]

In the 45 years since the inception of Civil Rights legislation in America, Democrats have taken blacks from the back of the Democrat bus, propelled them up to the front of the bus when the microphones and the cameras were present—exploiting their skin color—and then chucked them unceremoniously under the bus in order to get back what they consider their lost prejudice voters in the South. In other words, liberal Democrats have exploited people's race, holding alternating positions, all to increase their political power. And yet, this is the political party that consistently "earns" over 90% of black support at the polls?

Nancy Pelosi famously claimed to an un-skeptical press corps that she was going to "drain the swamp" of Washington corruption. The Democrats' ranks were rife with corruption under Pelosi's leadership and yet, her efforts to seek out the corrupt have caught no white members, while ensnaring a full 38 percent of the Congressional black Caucus.

According to David Freddoso of the *Washington Examiner* in 2010, writing about one of the many scandals plaguing Democrats, "PMA was shut down last year and raided by the FBI in the wake of several reports that its employees and clients were allegedly trading contributions for hundreds of millions of dollars in earmarks from certain members of Congress. This accusation has never been proven, and the Office of Congressional Ethics dropped its investigation last year."[70] The investigation was dropped—an investigation that would have netted half a dozen or so white Democrats for allegedly taking millions of dollars in bribes, making what Rangel and Jefferson had done look like petty theft by comparison. But that investigation was shut down by the very same "office of Congressional Ethics" that had taken up investigating black Democrats, and at a very suspicious time— right before the November elections. Pelosi isn't draining the swamp; she is holding Rangel's and Water's heads under the swamp water. According to the guidelines as established and aggressively heralded by Pelosi and the Liberal Left, the Demo-cratic Party is guilty, at minimum, of the "racial discrimination" they routinely assign to their political opposition.

But, if we apply the same standards that Pelosi and the Liber-al Left force American private businesses to adhere to, then what we are witness to is racism, pure and simple. If this was an affirmative action case, does anyone doubt that the evidence as presented would lead to a conviction? To believe otherwise would make you a racist by Democrat standards. This is what they have demanded from the rest of us for years.

For example, if you run a company and your employee base does not reflect the "racial make-up" of the community in which you are located, regardless of who has applied to work there, that is, according to federal standards, written by Democrats, evidence of racial discrimination. What if law enforcement arrests a disproportionate number of minorities? Again, the "evidence" is incontrovertible: Racial Discrimination. So, if the Democratic

Party engages in a "comprehensive effort" to rid its own body of corruption—a body that has long emitted the sights, sounds, smell of corruption—and then identifies only Black members, when they represent just a small percentage of the Democratic Congressional population? Well, apply the Democratic Party Racial Calculus, and you can only conclude Institutional Racism.

Democratic Party racism aside, this is not to suggest that Rangel, Waters, William Jefferson, etc. have been vindicated. But it is clear they were under the delusion that they, too, were free to participate in the wanton looting that has always firmly, if sort of quietly, defined the soul—the rich, liberal segregationist soul of the Democratic Party. It is now clear that they were never part of the "elite," and that no one bothered to tell them that "carte blanche" in the Democratic Party is delineated with a "hard c", as in blanc, for white. In other words, you do get a free pass, but only if you're rich, white, and liberal.

Pelosi and the Democratic Party have wielded the racial baton for years, silencing dissent, undermining opposition, engaging in the most egregious of personal attacks, and always for political ends. This is most often done without even the slightest bit of evidence.

"Evidence" was never important; the white liberal Democrats were the arbiters of what is and is not racism. In fact, how often does one hear that charge of racism now? How about every time a conservative defends States' Rights, declares affection for the 10th Amendment, or proposes opposition to ObamaCare?

But perhaps the Democrats' favorite tactic—aided and abetted by a sympathetic, sycophantic media—has always featured the slander of "unintentional racism," meaning someone could be guilty of racism, but not even conscious of it. This was also the most insidious of charges, because by its very nature it could not be accounted for—or defended against.

Well, Pelosi and her liberal leadership are guilty of much worse than even "unintentional racism." Their racism is active and pre-meditated. In fact, it was part of a much larger strategy to win back key Southern political districts. Abhorrent, for sure, and turned out to be a poorly calculated strategy. The Democrats' strategy of hanging their black members out as bait to bring out their historically racist constituency failed, because it likely doesn't even exist anymore. And can the media, the Congressional Black Caucus, and concerned Americans everywhere tolerate this disgusting racism any longer? Of all people, Democrats should be the most sensitive to this, given their party's history. In 2002, Professor Mackubin T. Owens wrote a reminder of the Democrat Party's roots: "Even the Civil Rights Act of 1964, which supposedly established the Democrats' bona fides on race, was passed in spite of the Democrats rather than because of them. Republican Senate Minority Leader Everett Dirksen pushed the bill through the Senate, despite the no-votes of 21 Democrats, including [Albert] Gore Sr. [father of former Vice President Gore] and Robert Byrd... In contrast, only four Republicans opposed the bill, mostly like Barry Goldwater on libertarian principles, not segregationist ones."[71]

As Owens points out, Democrats today have refused to advocate for a policy that is not only popular among blacks, but one that would actually help rectify previous injustices: "The single biggest obstacle to the achievement of true equality in the United States is not poverty, but education. If Democrats sincerely wished to help the minority children on whose behalf they claim to labor, they would embrace school choice to help such children escape the trap of sub-standard schools. But that would offend the teachers' unions upon which the Democrats depend for financial and "in-kind" support. So as has often been the case with the group politics of the Democratic Party, African-American interests are sacrificed to other groups who have more pull."

The nation may have thought this type of politics—surely the "Politics As Usual" historically practiced by the Democratic Party and subsequently decried by its leaders—were relics of the past. Unfortunately, what we have seen is the liberal elites exploit minorities for political power that benefits the white liberals. In her book Demonic, Ann Coulter captures what seem to be the real motivations of Democrats: "The liberal fairy tale that Southern bigots simply switched parties, from Democrat to Republican, is exactly wrong. What happened is: The Democrats switched mobs. Democrats will champion any group of hooligans in order to attain power. As Michael Barone said of the vicious segregationist (and Democrat) George Wallace, he was 'a man who really didn't believe in anything—a political opportunist who used opposition to integration to try and get himself ahead.' This is why the democrats are able to transition so seamlessly from defending Bull Connor racists to defending Black Panthers, hippies, yippies, Weathermen, feminists, Bush derangement syndrome liberals, Moveon.org, and every other indignant, angry mob."

What is most disturbing is how Democrats constantly get a free pass on race issues. Bill Clinton, for example, worked for, and was mentored by Senator J. William Fulbright, a Democrat from Arkansas. Fulbright was not only a segregationist but a signatory to the Southern Manifesto, a reaffirmation of segregation following the 1954 Brown vs. Board of Education Supreme Court decision. Upon Fulbright's death in 1995, while Clinton was president, he delivered the eulogy at Fulbright's funeral: "We come to celebrate and give thanks for the remarkable life of J. William Fulbright, a life that changed our country and our world forever and for the better..... In the work he did, the words he spoke and the life he lived, Bill Fulbright stood against the 20th Century's most destructive forces and fought to advance its brightest hopes."

Remember the public calls from Democrats demanding Clinton retract his high praise for a lifelong segregationist, and the outrage from the liberal media? Of course not, there were none. Not from the Democrats or from the media—which both have used every policy disagreement with Obama as evidence of racism. The mainstream media had a spasm of duplicity when it came to accusations of sexual misconduct against white liberal Bill Clinton and rumors about the "authentically" black Herman Cain, a Republican presidential candidate.

In eleven short years since Bill Clinton was president, the "one free grope rule" applied to Democrats turned into the liberal media in hot pursuit of second and the third generation rumors about a black conservative Republican. Anonymous claims of "[He] looked at me funny, and I think sex was on his mind," was all it took for the liberal media to come for Herman Cain with a rope. It started with *Politico*'s breathless reporting on Herman Cain over what would not have even been a notable Bill Clinton story. And it just so happened that it all came about just as Cain was moving into front-runner position for Republican nomination for president in the fall of 2011.

Remember when Clinton was running for president (and during his eight years in office) there were repeated allegations of affairs and serious evidence of sexual harassment, including "credible" evidence of rape? At that time, the media devoted most of their time to attacking anyone who mentioned Clinton's sordid past. The mainstream media were demanding at the time that the Special Prosecutor Ken Starr ignore Clinton's lying under oath about molesting an intern in the Oval Office so the nation could focus on more serious issues. If only Cain had used the liberal media's protection of Clinton for evidence far worse than even the rumors against an African American, he may have been able to drag liberal media hypocrisy on race out into the open.

Obama revealed his intentions to use race to divide the nation as well, except this time it was Latinos Obama sought to polarize. His nomination of Sonia Sotomayor to replace David Souter on the Supreme Court had all the obvious signs of playing racial politics. He could have nominated a qualified and acceptable candidate for the Supreme Court who would have, regardless of the person's race or gender, had bipartisan support. But instead of rising above partisan politics and delivering the "change" he promised during the campaign, he called a play right out of the standard Democrats' dirty tricks playbook: the race hustle.

The mainstream media did their part by reading directly from the Democrat talking points and repeatedly added the White House manufactured line "How can Republicans oppose Sonia Sotomayor without alienating Hispanics?" What an awful insult to the Hispanic community to suggest that their interests are no deeper than the color of someone's skin. Sotomayor's views were known to be based on the Far Left, including making law from the bench, and saying that her being "a wise Latina" better qualified her to interpret the law than a man. How sad it is that Obama would select someone whose judicial views are so antithetical to the constitution and then use that person's race to divide the country for his political benefit.

So concerned was the Obama administration about a close examination of Sotomayor's judicial record, White House press secretary Robert Gibbs issued this warning: "I think it is probably important for anybody involved in this debate to be exceedingly careful with the way in which they've decided to describe different aspects of this impending confirmation," signaling that any opposition to Sotomayor's nomination would be considered anti-Hispanic.

Obama has said that "his judges" would have "that quality of empathy, of understanding and identifying with people's hopes and struggles." Obama said, "I will seek someone who understands that justice isn't about some abstract legal theory." So there you have it; to Obama, the law of the land is "an abstract legal theory" not to get in the way of his agenda.

A chilling January 2001 interview reveals what far-reaching consequences Obama-styled "empathy" can have for the rule of law and the US Constitution: "The Supreme Court never ventured into the issues of redistribution of wealth and sort of more basic issues of political and economic justice in this society," Obama told an interviewer for a Chicago radio station. Obama went on to complain that when ultra-liberal, judicial activist Earl Warren was chief justice of the Supreme Court "it didn't break free from the essential constraints that were placed by the founding fathers in the Constitution." He seems to really miss that the whole point of the Constitution was to prevent tyrants from "break[ing] free" from the rule of law and declaring themselves the final arbiters of what is legal. But, then again, maybe he doesn't miss that point at all. In the grand scheme of things, Sotomayor seems a perfect fit for Obama. She has already declared that her biases as a "Latina woman" are superior to her white male counterparts. To Obama and Sotomayor the Consti-

159

tution is only a temporary impediment to their "empathetic" nirvana.

Everyone, especially Hispanics, should be outraged by this cynical exploitation of race by the Obama administration. Obama has cleverly diffused outrage by doing so many outrageous things across a wide spectrum. When you take the race-baiting and class-warfare away from Democrats and the liberal media, all that is left is raw anti-Americanism.

Chapter 15

Race, Religion, and Power

Obama was the perfect candidate for Democrats because his presidency played to their objectives. Obama already agreed with the Democrat agenda of consolidating power in Washington, and there was a bonus: He had the right skin color. During his first two years in office Democrats and the media frequently cited racism as the reason for opposition to Obama's policies. It would take several books to document all such cases, but here are a few examples:

"What is it about this president that has stripped away the veneer of respect that normally accompanies the office of the President? Why do Republicans think this president is unpresidential...? It could be the economic times, it could be that he won so big in 2008 or, let's face it, the color of his skin."

-- *MSNBC* contributor Richard Wolffe

"I think that a lot of what the president has experienced is because he's black...You know, whether it's questioning his intellect or whether or not he's Ivy League. It's always either he's not educated enough or he's too educated; or he's too black or he's not black enough; he's too Christian or not Christian enough. There are all these things where he has to walk this very fine line to even be successful."

-- Angela Rye, Executive Director of the Congressional Black Caucus

"I think an overwhelming portion of the intensely demon-strated animosity toward President Barack Obama is based on the fact that he is a black man, that he's African American."

-- Former President Jimmy Carter

"But ask yourself when you next go to a Tea Party rally, or watch one on television, or listen to a politician or a commenta-tor praise these things or merely treat them as if it was just a coincidence that they are virtually segregated. Ask yourself: Where are the black faces? Who am I marching with? What are we afraid of? And if it really is only a president's policy and not his skin."

-- Keith Olbermann, *MSNBC*

Beyond the phony outrage is the fact that Obama's signature achievement, and also that which generated the most outrage from the general public, was his healthcare bill. If Americans opposed Obama's healthcare bill because he is half black, what motivated the public outrage over government-run healthcare when Bill Clinton proposed it in the 1990s? Clinton worked for—and admired—a segregationist, J. William Fulbright. Many of the Democrats' leading lights of the 20th century had two things in common: they believed in the utopian society (that is that the brightest among us should rule over all of us), and they were segregationists. Democrats have no reservation about celebrating J. William Fulbright, Woodrow Wilson, and Franklin Roosevelt because they all believed in the same thing. The utopian society run by "masterminds" as described in Mark Levin's book Ameritopia: "The mastermind is driven by his own boundless conceit and delusional aspirations, which he self-identifies as a noble calling. He alone is uniquely qualified to carry out this mission. He is, in his own mind, a savior of mankind, if only man will bend to his own will."

This is further evidence that defending people from racial discrimination has nothing to do with the liberal's real objective. Using the politics of race, however, is a way for liberals to get power. How else to explain the Democrat's and liberal media's obsession with appeasing Muslim extremists, and their insistence that every Muslim is peace-loving and condemns violence even when they refuse to condemn Islamic terrorism? The Judeo-Christian ethic, on which Western civilization is based, is constantly under assault from the Left despite its tolerance for all of the boutique causes de guerre of the Left. Muslim extremists, on the other hand, violently oppose everything liberals hold sacred, except for the destruction of the tolerant Judeo-Christian West.

There have been more angry attacks on Americans from the so-called peaceful Muslim world for the accidental burning of a few Korans that were in U.S. possession than we ever heard from them in condemning their fellow Muslims for perpetrating terrorist attacks on behalf of their religion. In February 2012, it was revealed that military personnel inadvertently burned some Korans along with other materials. Based on the reaction from Muslims, and liberals in the U.S., you would have thought that the soldiers burned actual Muslim people. But they, of course, didn't. It was just books. The *New York Times* reported on March 2, 2012 that soldiers risking their lives to protect American national security are under investigation and face serious penalties for the mistake: "Even as Americans have raced to ease Afghan outrage over the burning, releasing information on Friday that American service members could face disciplinary action, accounts from more than a dozen Americans and Afghans involved in investigating the incineration laid out a complex string of events that will do little to assuage an Afghan public that in some quarters has called for deaths to avenge the sacrilege."[72]

This is a country that refused to turn over Osama bin Laden after he burned three thousand American citizens, who are demanding the deaths of soldiers who accidentally burned a few Muslim books. In the summer of 2010, the threat by Florida pastor Terry Jones that he was going to burn Korans on the tenth anniversary of September 11, 2001 led to the deaths of twenty people around the world. Many Muslims and liberals demanded that Jones repent of this wickedness so as not to offend the global Muslim community. Among those who called for Jones, and the rest of us, to not offend Muslims was none other than Feisal Abdul Rauf, the Imam leading the effort to build the Ground Zero Mosque no matter how many Americans were offended.

In a 1,000-word op-ed in the *New York Times*, Rauf dismissed the concerns of 70 percent of America, labeling us "radicals." Rauf gave short, arrogant shrift to the victims' families, and he refused to denounce his own vitriolic statements regarding the U.S. in the aftermath of 9/11. Rauf had previously claimed that America's policies were an "accomplice" to the slaughter of 9/11, and said "the U.S. must acknowledge the harm they have done to Muslims before the terror can stop." Rauf did something else in his *Times* op-ed—he subtly threatened Americans with more violence if his Ground Zero Mosque location was moved away from the site of the devastating attacks: "These efforts by radicals at distortion, endanger our national security and the personal security of Americans worldwide... Americans must not back away from completion of this project. If we do, we cede the discourse and, essentially, our future to radicals on both sides."[73]

There were no Korans burned nor mosques opposed before the Islamic terrorists murdered nearly three thousand Americans. And yet, we are not supposed to burn the book they say inspired them to do it—or there will be more violence—Obama and Hillary Clinton tell us. Let's get this straight: not burning the Koran led to the burning of nearly three thousand Americans. And now, burning the Koran, we are told, will lead to more Americans dying? Obama and Hillary Clinton want to abrogate the First Amendment in order to mollify Muslims who are threatening violence. That will surely teach those "radicals" who is winning the war on terrorism.

Killing unborn children causes violence too, and not only to the murdered children themselves it turns out; the occasional abortion provider finds himself in danger as well. So, the same lunatics demanding that the First Amendment be trampled in order to shield Islamists from the slightest offense are the very ones loudly declaring that the right to kill unborn babies is so sacrosanct they must send federal marshals out to protect the abortionists. It's a shock some of these Democrats can even walk straight and upright, so contorted they become defending their so-called "principles."

When Muslims threaten violence in response to any Constitutionally-protected act, the proper response should be to multiply those acts to demonstrate that this country is governed by laws, not fear. And wasn't that the exact lecture they—the "peaceful" Imam and his wife, and all the newly minted Leftist First Amendment stalwarts—gave us about the Ground Zero mosque?

The media and the Democrats have labeled Tea Partiers as violent and racist due to the alleged paper signs they carry. However, these elitists refuse to use the same filter of condemnation when talking about the Muslim faith and the murderous actions of the 19 Muslim hijackers on 9/11, or the Muslim underwear bomber on New Year's Day, or the Muslim Fort Hood attacker, or the Muslim Times Square bomber, or any other Muslims like Osama Bin Laden, the rest of Al Qaeda, Hamas and the Taliban. In fact, anyone opposed to the Ground Zero Mosque, Tea Partier or not, is labeled insensitive, ignorant and racist.

The Left has attacked Christianity for decades and has succeeded largely in taking discussions of G-d out of public school classrooms, ensured the Pledge of Allegiance is rarely recited, and sued to have "In G-d We Trust" taken off of the U.S. currency. How ironic they are the first to stand up and fight for the Muslim faith. Anyone with even peripheral knowledge of the Muslim faith and Sharia Law understands how absurd it is for the Left— self-heralding champions of the feminist movement and the pushers of "gay marriage"—to adopt this charge, especially in light of how Muslims believe women and homosexuals should be dealt with—that is to say, killing homosexuals and treating women as chattel.

Since the liberals advocate bowing to the threat of Islamic violence, here is a thought: Consider how the Democrats are constantly telling us how dangerous the Tea Partiers are and the media wailing shrill warnings that Tea Partiers are on the tipping point of violence, so to be consistent shouldn't liberals then advocate for lower taxes, a halt in spending, and a hurry-up-and-appease the dangerous Tea Party protestors approach before someone gets hurt?

Once again, the Left has constructed a box, tied themselves in knots, and climbed right in; they either really believe in appeasing dangerous people, or they have been lying about how dangerous they think the Tea Partiers are.

The odd thing about the Ground Zero Mosque is that it unites belligerent Islamists and the Elitist Far Left on one side against the rest of America. This dichotomy illustrates perfectly my analysis from 2004: The only thing that radical Islam and the Left have in common is their mutual hatred of the United States. The Left hates America so much they are willing to unite with a religion that is the actuality of all that they claim to hate about Christianity in order to destroy Christianity. After 40 years of trampling on freedom of religion, the Left has now embraced it as the Holy Grail of America's greatness. Quick, start praying in schools before they change their minds.

Pelosi and the rest of the Democrats, including Obama, were terrified of the Ground Zero Mosque issue because it put them in a box right before the 2010 election, the time at which Democrats prefer to hide their anti-Americanism, and pretend they, too, believe in freedom and Judeo-Christian values. The mosque issue was a simple, up-or-down question that made it even more problematic for the Democrats because there is no room to obfuscate on the issue.

Obama tried it and came out looking like a fool, first by endorsing the mosque and then saying that the endorsement was only for the First Amendment. How clever. But we already knew where Obama stood before he put his foot in his mouth; he always takes the side of the Muslims over that of Americans, whether in his outrageous apologies for the crimes he imagines we've committed against Islam, or by doling out our tax money to fund the terrorist group Hamas.

Obama created a new paradox for the media. Usually, the media and Democrats deride Christians for being narrow minded and bigoted. Obama himself has even mocked Christians, even if it was in his very awkward, inaccurate way: "And even if we did

167

have only Christians in our midst, if we expelled every non-Christian from the United States of America, whose Christianity would we teach in the schools? Would we go with James Dobson's, or Al Sharpton's? Which passages of Scripture should guide our public policy? Should we go with Leviticus, which suggests slavery is ok and that eating shellfish is abomination? How about Deuteronomy, which suggests stoning your child if he strays from the faith?"

Obama apparently did not cite the television show, "The West Wing," which used the same concept in an October 2000 broadcast. Martin Sheen, who played President Josiah Bartlet on the show, lectured a Jewish radio talk show host in a demeaning way about the application of Hebrew scripture in modern society. The bizarre thing about Obama's lifting of Sheen's work is that the Sheen character quoted Hebrew scripture to a Jewish woman; Obama quoted Hebrew Law Scripture to Christians. Someone needs to explain to Obama that Christians don't believe that the Hebrew law applies to them. Fortunately for Obama, there is nothing in the New Testament about penalties for a president being a hack, and not understanding Greek scripture, the Holy Book of the faith that he claims as his own.

Paradoxically, the Democrats and the media who are harsh in their judgment of most Christians are exactly the opposite when it comes to Obama. For some reason Obama's Christian faith is better, and while the media is constantly carping about what a great and peaceful religion Islam is, they attack anyone who dares to notice Obama's affinity for it. In August 2010, the *Washington Post* portrayed Obama as a victim of gossip regarding religion without noticing that Obama himself has done much to contribute to the ambiguity: "The president's religion, like his place of birth, has been the subject of Internet-spread rumors and falsehoods since before he began his presidential campaign, and the poll indicates that those rumors have gained currency since Obama took office. The number of people who now correctly identify Obama as a Christian has dropped to 34 percent, down from nearly half when he took office."[74]

The so-called "mainstream media" has spent years trying to determine how anywhere from one-fifth to one-quarter of the American people could conclude that President Obama is a Muslim. The *Post*'s and other "news" outlets have almost universally condemned Americans as "ignorant," "ill-informed," "racist," or "bigoted," asserting disdainfully that it's "obvious" that Obama is a Christian. "Obvious?" What has been obvious is what the media has overlooked: themselves, President Obama, and Muslims.

Author and proud Muslim, Asma Gull Hasan, wrote in the February 2009 issue of *Forbes Magazine* that "since Election Day, I have been part of more and more conversations with Muslims in which it was either offhandedly agreed that Obama is Muslim or enthusiastically blurted out. In commenting on our new president, 'I have to support my fellow Muslim brother,' would slip out of my mouth before I had a chance to think twice."

But the mainstream media mocks the increasing number of Americans who believe Obama is a Muslim. Because those Americans are in agreement with these Muslims, does this make the Muslims bigoted for being in agreement with conservatives, or the media bigoted for casting their defense of Obama so wide that it snared one of their favorite groups worthy of protection?

The media should have been searching themselves rather than accusing others; had they done their job investigating Barack Obama during the 2008 campaign, Americans might have a better handle on even the basic dimensions of America's 44th president.

But the media completely abdicated its responsibility, failing to provide any coverage skeptical of the Obama campaign's own tightly scripted narrative, a narrative that many Americans saw right through, which may be why the media elites are so agitated.

So invested were they in Obama's victory, the mainstream media ignored, or in some cases actively suppressed, any story lines that called into question Obama's fitness for office—this included his shocking lack of experience; his decades-long association with domestic terrorists Bill Ayers and Bernadine Dohrn; his anti-American and anti-Semitic "minister," Jeremiah Wright; and his relationship with now-convicted tax-evader and all-around sleazy character Tony Rezko. Nor did the mainstream media call into question his links to radical Islam supporters such as Rashid Khalidi.

Remember, this is the media that so thoroughly browbeat a third-tier surrogate of the McCain campaign for referring to "Barack Hussein Obama," that John McCain himself subsequently declared, publicly, that his opponent's middle name was henceforth off limits. Perhaps Obama should have stuck with his groovy, 70s moniker, "Barry", that he jettisoned when it became politically advantageous for him to adopt "Barack" as his ethnic-novelty name.

Nothing earned the media's contempt during the 2008 election quite like the suggestion, however muted, that Obama might be a Muslim—or might harbor Socialist ideals. Any purveyor of such outlandish rumors was met with fierce derision—even after Obama was filmed declaring his intention to "spread the wealth around," and also after he was taped at a wine and cheese party in San Francisco attacking Christians for "clinging to their guns and religion."

So miserably deficient was the campaign coverage—and so deficient has been the ongoing "investigative" coverage of the man in office—that the American people have simply been left to fill the void on their own, with only their interpretation of Obama's distortions and fabrications about Islam's greatness.

Obama's actions have led many Americans to conclude that he could be Muslim. Who can blame them? Not only did he declare that America was no longer a Christian nation, but he also claimed that America is one of the world's largest Muslim nations. He supports the Ground Zero Mosque, and in his first book <u>Dreams from My Father</u>, he stated that, if political winds turn against Muslims, he "will stand with them". Also, it is significant that he refuses to acknowledge that radical Islam has declared war against us.

It isn't just Obama's overt Islamic advocacy. It's also that so many Americans have come to recognize his inherent dishonesty. They no longer trust him because he smears his critics with outrageous falsehoods, with the hope that he'll polarize the majority of people in his direction. Fortunately, he underestimated Americans' distrust of his fawning allies in the mainstream media.

Americans' distrust of the media is so deep that if the media insists that Obama is a Christian, then a sizeable segment will automatically embrace the exact opposite position. So when the *Washington Post* demanded that Obama is obviously a Christian, the majority of the relative few who read it must have immediately concluded there was a good reason to believe otherwise. Ironically, the "obvious" reason in the mind of liberal journalists that Obama is a Christian was the twenty years he spent in Jeremiah Wright's church—the very exculpatory evidence they could not touch because it would have tainted Obama with Wright's extremist anti-American views.

Despite all the noise, diversion, and debate, Obama may not be a Muslim. But, if the liberal media really believed he was a Christian wouldn't they ridicule him like they do others that call themselves Christians? President George W. Bush was frequently ridiculed by media figures for his faith, such as when *New York Times Magazine* writer Ron Suskind repeatedly implied that Bush's religion was not "reality based." And yet Obama, whose religion dangled precariously by a thread—the other end of which was held by Jeremiah Wright—was never asked embarrassing questions about how his faith would affect his ability to govern.

Did the media believe that Obama's faith was a matter of political convenience? The difference in the treatment of Bush's faith versus Obama's is similar to their approach to defending Islamism. The liberal's attraction to Islam is consistent with its attraction to all other disparate causes. That is, it provides them with victims, even when they must create them, which they can use to tear down their political opponents to defend the power of the increasingly secular state run almost entirely by white liberals.

The very essence of the Faustian bargain that liberals offer to minority groups and grievance agitators is their political power in exchange for money appropriated from the productive people who provide the aggrieved with the opportunity to liberate themselves. Liberal Democrat proposals are never rooted in the principles they espouse. If only rich people could vote, Democrats would not argue for a minimum wage, instead they would lecture the poor about how it is their patriotic duty to provide cheap labor for wealthy business owners. The liberal's so-called principles are rooted in wherever they can extract coercive political power for themselves.

Conclusion

For many years progressives have demoted freedom and promoted their idea of a virtuous government -- and now even more so under Barack Obama. For years the Left has attacked and maligned the common morality of mainstream America while forcing their extremist morality on us and calling it "public policy". In 2009 many Americans finally had had enough, and they took to the streets to have their voices heard. When they did, the very progressives who for decades celebrated and encouraged every form of protest and demonstration, attacked the very Americans who for years had been quietly paying for those streets -- insulting and accusing them of the unthinkable while having the hubris to claim that they stand for the people who "play by the rules".

The catalyst which drove the protests was the notion that Obama was declaring that he had the authority to take money from some, at the point of a gun, to pay for someone else's healthcare. But it really wasn't as much about the healthcare bill as much as it was about the idea that Obama and the Democrats had awarded themselves the authority to do it, and thus changing the character of the freest and most prosperous nation in the history of civilization. Americans who truly love their country are now face to face with the one promoting its decline.

About the Author

Scott Wheeler is a prolific investigative reporter, having written two books and worked in many mediums as a newspaper reporter and editor, as well as chief correspondent for *American Investigator Television Magazine*. As a filmmaker he has produced 17 television documentaries, and has consulted on more than a dozen others.

As an expert analyst on political issues as well as national security matters, he frequently appears on *Fox News Channel*, *Fox Business Channel*, *MSNBC*, *CNN*, *BBC* and *CNBC*, as well as other national and international programs. Wheeler is currently the Executive Director of the National Republican Trust PAC, and Director of National Investigative Media.

Wheeler is a veteran of the U.S. Army Infantry.

References

Part I

Chapter 1

[1] Tapper, Jake. *ABC News.* "Obama Apologizes for Saying Troops' Lives 'Wasted'".
<http://abcnews.go.com/Politics/story?id=2872135&page=1#.UDUNP8Fl Qxg>. 13 Feb. 2007.

[2] Zeleny, Jeff. *The New York Times.* "Leading Democrat in Senate Tells Reporters, 'This War Is Lost'".
<http://www.nytimes.com/2007/04/20/washington/20cong.html>. 20 Apr. 2007.

[3] Yen, Hope. *Associated Press.* "Open Government Advocates Praise Obama Move Toward Greater Disclosure of Agency Information".
<http://www.startribune.com/templates/Print_This_Story?sid=38031349>. 22 Jan. 2009.

[4] Ibid.

[5] Ibid.

[6] Mazetti, Mark and Scott Shane. *The New York Times.* "Interrogation Memos Detail Harsh Tactics by the C.I.A.".
<http://www.nytimes.com/2009/04/17/us/politics/17detain.html?pagewant ed=all>. 16 Apr. 2009

Chapter 2

[7] Sheridan, Mary Beth ; Markon, Jerry and DeYoung, Karen. *The Washington Post.* "Suburban Spies Russia-bound in Cold War-style Swap".
<http://www.statesman.com/news/world/suburban-spies-russia-bound-in-cold-war-style-793152.html?printArticle=y>. 8 Jul. 2010.

[8] Van Cleave, Michelle. *The Wall Street Journal.* "Michelle Van Cleave: Russian Spies Haven't Gone Away."
<http://online.wsj.com/article/SB10001424052702304299304577347583937 893526.html>. 20 Apr. 2012.

[9] Sheridan, Mary Beth and Jerry Markon. *The Washington* Post. <http://www.washingtonpost.com/wp-dyn/content/article/2010/07/08/AR2010070803476_2.html?wprss=rss_worl d/europe&sid=ST2010070702502>. 9 Jul. 2010.

[10] Ibid.

[11] Ibid.

[12] Ibid.

[13] Ibid.

[14] *Agence France-Presse*. "U.S. to Cease Observing Arms Treaty with Russia: State Dept". <http://www.rawstory.com/rs/2011/11/22/u-s-to-cease-observing-arms-treaty-with-russia-state-dept/>. 22 Nov. 2011

[15] *Fox News*. "Polish, Czech Officials Slam Obama's Missile Defense Shift as a Betrayal". <http://www.foxnews.com/world/2009/09/18/polish-czech-officials-slam-obamas-missile-defense-shift-betrayal/>. 18 Sep. 2009.

[16] Gertz, Bill. *The Washington Times*. <http://www.washingtontimes.com/news/2012/jan/4/inside-the-ring-215329133/?page=all>. 4 Jan. 2012.

[17] Ibid.

Chapter 3

[18] Robertson, Matthew. *The Epoch Times*. "Chinese Pianist Plays Propaganda Tune at White House". <http://www.theepochtimes.com/n2/united-states/propaganda-white-house-lang-lang-49822-all.html>. 22 Jan. 2011.

[19] Wilson, Scott. *The Washington Post*. "Despite Risks, Obama Ready to Press China on Human Rights". <http://www.washingtonpost.com/wp-dyn/content/article/2011/01/14/AR2011011406907.html>. 15 Jan. 2011.

Chapter 4

[20] *Agence France Presse.* "Hamas Leader Hails Obama's New Approach". <http://www.google.com/hostednews/afp/article/ALeqM5j2gvclboeIPtpN9 ZtLudBog3HNgw>. 22 Mar. 2009

[21] *Al Arabiyya News.* "Obama Tells Al Arabiya Peace Talks Should Resume". <http://www.alarabiya.net/articles/2009/01/27/65087.html>. 27 Jan. 2009.

[22] Bronner, Ethan. *The New York Times.* "New Israeli Tack Needed on Gaza, U.S. Officials Say". <http://www.nytimes.com/2010/06/03/world/middleeast/03policy.html>. 2 Jun. 2010.

[23] Cooper, Helene and Isabel Kershner. *The New York Times.* "Obama Pledges New Aid to Palestinians". <http://www.nytimes.com/2010/06/10/world/middleeast/10prexy.html>. 9 Jun . 2010.

[24] Ibid.

[25] Ibid.

[26] McCarthy, Andrew. *National Review Online.* "Obama Pal Rashid Khalidi Back in the News for Aiding Hamas". <http://www.nationalreview.com/corner/233418/obama-pal-rashid-khalidi-back-news-aiding-hamas-andrew-c-mccarthy#>. 20 Jul. 2010

[27] Ibid.

[28] The Organizers Forum. <http://organizersforum.org/page/3/>. 25 May 2011.

[29] *Fox News.* Muslim Brotherhood Members to Attend Obama's Cairo Speech. <http://www.foxnews.com/politics/2009/06/03/muslim-brotherhood-members-attend-obamas-cairo-speech/#ixzz24IwKUbvX>. 3 Jun. 2009.

Chapter 5

[30] The Middle East Media Research Institute. <http://www.memri.org/report/en/print2806.htm>. 16 Jun. 2008.

[31] Ibid.

[32] Ibid.

[33] Benn, Aluf. *Haaretz.* "Will Obama's Denuclearization Plan Mean 'Dimona for Natanz'?". <http://www.haaretz.com/print-edition/news/will-obama-s-denuclearization-plan-mean-dimona-for-natanz-1.275517>. 7 May 2009.

[34] Wong, Kristina. *ABC News.* The Emergence of President Obama's Muslim Roots. <http://abcnews.go.com/blogs/politics/2009/06/abc-news-jake-tapper-and-sunlen-miller-report-the-other-day-we-heard-a-comment-from-a-white-house-aide-that-neverwould-have/>. 2 Jun. 2009.

[35] Lichtblau, Eric. *The New York Times.* "Justice Dept. Backs Saudi Royal Family on 9/11 Lawsuit". <http://www.nytimes.com/2009/05/30/us/politics/30families.html>. 29 May 2009.

[36] Mukasey, Michael. *The Wall Street* Journal. "Michael Mukasey: Obama and the bin Laden Bragging Rights". <http://online.wsj.com/article/SB1000142405270230391690457737455254630 8474.html>. 30 Apr. 2012.

[37] Graham-Harrison, Emma and Rajeev Syal. *The Guardian.* "Taliban infiltration fears grow as 'rogue' Afghan police gun down British soldiers". <http://www.guardian.co.uk/world/2012/may/13/taliban-fears-afghan-police-british-soldiers>. 13 May 2012.

[38] *CBS News.* "Marines to Lead Obama's Afghanistan Surge". <http://www.cbsnews.com/8301-250_162-5846260.html>. 1 Dec. 2009.

[39] Hastings, Michael. *Rolling Stone.* "The Runaway General". <http://www.rollingstone.com/politics/news/the-runaway-general-20100622>. 22 Jun. 2010.

Chapter 6

Part II

Chapter 7

[40] Kuhn, David Paul. *Real Clear Politics.* "Wall Street Turns On Dems". <http://www.realclearpolitics.com/articles/2010/04/30/wall_street_turns_o n_dems__105380.html>. 30 Apr. 2010.

[41] Ibid.

[42] *Reuters.* "U.S. banking laws unable to stop JPMorgan loss: Republican Boehner". <http://in.mobile.reuters.com/article/businessNews/idINDEE84J07S20120 520> . 20 May 2012.

[43] *Politico.* <http://dyn.politico.com/members/forums/thread.cfm?catid=1&subcatid=1 &threadid=3996749#3996749>. 28 Apr. 2010.

Chapter 8

Chapter 9

[44] Calmes, Jackie and Nicholas Kulish. *The New York Times*"Weak Economy Points to Obama's Constraints". <http://www.nytimes.com/2012/06/03/us/politics/obamas-hands-tied-on-weak-economy.html?pagewanted=all>. 2 Jun. 2012.

Part III

Chapter 10

[45] Obama, Barack. *The Washington Post.* "The Action Americans Need". <http://www.washingtonpost.com/wp-dyn/content/article/2009/02/04/AR2009020403174.html>. 5 Feb. 2009.

[46] Ibid.

[47] Seib, Gerald F. *The Wall Street Journal.* "In Crisis, Opportunity for Obama". <http://online.wsj.com/article/SB122721278056345271.html>. 21 Nov. 2008.

[48] Obama, Barack. The Washington Post. "The Action Americans Need". <http://www.washingtonpost.com/wp-dyn/content/article/2009/02/04/AR2009020403174.html>. 5 Feb. 2009.

[49] Brecht Forum. "The New York Marxist School".
<http://brechtforum.org/nyms>.

[50] Dwyer, Devin. *ABC News.* "Obama: Occupy Wall Street 'Not That Different' From Tea Party Protests".
<http://abcnews.go.com/blogs/politics/2011/10/obama-occupy-wall-street-not-that-different-from-tea-party-protests/>. 18 Oct. 2012.

[51] *Politico.* "Obama Knock 'Certain News Channels'".
<http://www.politico.com/blogs/michaelcalderone/0409/Obama_knocks_certain_news_channels.html>. 29 Apr. 2009.

Chapter 11

[52] Ikenson, Daniel J. The Cato Institute.
<http://www.cato.org/publications/congressional-testimony/lasting-implications-general-motors-bailout>. 22 Jun. 2011.

[53] Ibid.

[54] Ibid.

[55] Cook, Theresa. *ABC News.* "White House Denies Charge By Attorney that Administration Threatened to Destroy Investment Firm's Reputation".
<http://abcnews.go.com/blogs/politics/2009/05/bankruptcy-atto/>. 2 May 2009.

[56] *ABC News.* "President Obama irked by creditors".
<http://abcnews.go.com/Business/story?id=7476106&page=1#.UDVGeMFlQxg>.

[57] Flint, Jerry. *Forbes.com.* "The Steal Of The Century".
<http://www.forbes.com/2009/01/31/chrysler-fiat-autos-business-manufacturing_0131_flint.html>. 31 Jan. 2009.

[58] Emmanuel, Ezekiel. *The Lancet.* "Evaluating the Principles for Allocating Scarce Medical Interventions."
<http://www.law.harvard.edu/programs/petrie-flom/workshop/pdf/emanuel.pdf>. 31 Jan. 2009.

[59] Turner, Gracie-Marie. *The Washington Examiner*. "Obamacare's six worst flaws". <http://washingtonexaminer.com/article/36955>. 8 Jul. 2009.

[60] Sack, Kevin and Marjorie Connelly. *The New York Times*. "In Poll, Wide Support for Government-Run Health". <http://www.nytimes.com/2009/06/21/health/policy/21poll.html>. 20 Jun. 2009.

Part IV

Chapter 12

[61] *Pew Research Center Publications*. "Partisan Gap in Obama Job Approval Widest in Modern Era" <http://pewresearch.org/pubs/1178/polarized-partisan-gap-in-obama-approval-historic>. 2 Apr. 2009.

Chapter 13

[62] Sidoti, Liz and Jennifer Agiesta. *Associated Press*. <http://www.huffingtonpost.com/2011/05/11/obama-approval-rating-_n_860409.html>. 11 May 2011.

[63] Yost, Pete. *Associated Press*. "McCain linked to group in Iran-Contra affair". <http://www.usatoday.com/news/topstories/2008-10-07-761883650_x.htm >. 7 Oct. 2008.

[64] Ibid.

[65] Barstow, David. *The New York Times*. "Tea Party Lights Fuse for Rebellion on Right". <http://www.nytimes.com/2010/02/16/us/politics/16teaparty.html?_r=1>. 15 Feb. 2010.

[66] O'Driscoll, Gerald. *The Wall Street Journal*. "The Federal Reserve's Covert Bailout of Europe". <http://online.wsj.com/article/SB10001424052970204464404577118682763082876.html>. 28 Dec. 2011.

[67] Barstow, David. The New York Times. "Tea Party Lights Fuse for Rebellion on Right".

<http://www.nytimes.com/2010/02/16/us/politics/16teaparty.html?_r=1>. 15 Feb. 2010.

[68] Ibid.

Chapter 14

[69] Harrop, Froma. *Real Clear Politics*. "Ethics Trials May Help, Not Hurt, Democrats". <http://www.realclearpolitics.com/articles/2010/08/06/ethics_trials_may_help_not_hurt_democrats_106643.html>. 6 Aug. 2010.

[70] Wheeler, Scott and Buckley Carlson. *The Daily Caller*. "The Democrats' new/old southern strategy". <http://dailycaller.com/2010/08/09/the-democrats-newold-southern-strategy/> 9 Aug. 2010.

[71] Owens, Mackubin T. Ashbrook Center at Ashland University. "The Democratic Party's Legacy of Racism". <http://ashbrook.org/publications/oped-owens-02-racism/>. Dec. 2002.

Chapter 15

[72] Rubin, Alissa J. *The New York Times*. "Chain of Avoidable Errors Cited in Koran Burning". <http://www.nytimes.com/2012/03/03/world/asia/5-soldiers-are-said-to-face-punishment-in-koran-burning-in-afghanistan.html?pagewanted=all>. 2 Mar. 2012

[73] Rauf, Feisal Abdul. *The New York Times*. "Building on Faith". <http://www.nytimes.com/2010/09/08/opinion/08mosque.html>. 7 Sep. 2010.

[74] Cohen, Jon and Michael D. Shear. *The Washington Post*. "Poll shows more Americans think Obama is a Muslim". <http://www.washingtonpost.com/wp-dyn/content/article/2010/08/18/AR2010081806913.html>. 19 Aug. 2010.